TOMATO PASTE LEADERSHIP

The Secret Sauce to Growth, Profit, and Time for What Matters

Domenic A. Chiarella

Tomato Paste Leadership

tla
pub

Published by Thought Leader Academy Publishing

3901 North Kildare Ave

Chicago, IL | 60641

ISBN: 979-8-9922574-5-8

Table of Contents

Acknowledgments

I want to extend my heartfelt gratitude to my wife, Rosemary, who has been my unwavering source of strength, understanding, and love for over forty years, supporting me through every new endeavor.

To my daughters, Toni Marie, Rachael, and Jessica, your boundless energy for life and constant inspiration have guided me through every challenge and triumph.

I am also immensely grateful to my favorite mother-in-law (my only, but still my favorite), Annunziatina, whose life experience and Italian wisdom ignited the idea for this book.

The support of all the remarkable women in my life has been the driving force behind this endeavor.

Lastly, I thank my first mentors, my mom and dad: "The General" Anna, and "The Full Colonel" John. They are forever in my heart and soul, looking down from heaven and watching over me.

A Letter from Domenic

I am humbled, fortunate, and grateful to everyone I've encountered along my business journey. With these family, friends, associations, coaches, and employees, I went from an eager owner-worker to a strategic leader of a thriving $15 million organization in the top three percent of my industry.

I changed the names of the innocent and not-so-innocent in these stories I will share with you. But I am so proud of everyone I've worked and collaborated with. I'm proud to tell you about them because I have been blessed to create one of the most creative, substantial organizations alongside them. We grew together. I mentored and taught them. I created systems and strategies for them. I nurtured them and listened to their ideas. In return, they grew beyond what I ever taught them, achieving success on their own.

I cherish the thought that I contributed to their success. I helped create an environment where they could thrive, and because of their strengths and values, they could step into that environment, and we could make something unique. Boy, did we ever. I don't know what I would have done without every person in this book. I've changed the names of the few cautionary stories to protect privacy. I learned just as much from those people, and I appreciate them and wish them well.

Dear reader, I write these stories and methods for you—the business owner and entrepreneur who knows there's more to life and business. I know you want to discover how to grow your company and be more successful for your employees, clients, and families. I offer my stories, growth successes, learning failures, and proven strategies to help you along your journey as you transform yourself and your organization just as I did.

My goal is to use the grace and opportunities God has blessed me with and, as my dad taught me, "to make this world a little better."

My dad, a man of many sayings, used to say, "I is an engineer." He would say this whenever something was outside his talents. He would then take the time to learn and make it happen. Like my father, I is a computer engineer. Writing a book is outside my talents, but I found mentors and invested the time to make it happen. This book is another learning experience.

I am feeling it.

Feeling the energy inside me.

Waiting for it to come out.

Time seems to march on.

Still, I am as young as I will ever be today.

I will make art.

Find a way to be more.

Share more.

Focus on the beauty of life.

The ones that I want in my life.

It is our gift.

The journey continues.

—Domenic A Chiarella

Prologue

"The truth is not for all men, but only for those who seek it."

—Ayn Rand

It was January, during a freezing winter, on a Monday morning.

I was sitting at my desk working on a new work order and invoice system for the spring when I looked up.

My production manager, Julio, was standing by the door.

He had a glimmer in his eyes.

"Domenic, there is a pending nor'easter snowstorm moving into New England at the end of the week. The forecast calls for at least two days of snow, sleet, and chaos." He smiled when he said, "They're forecasting eighteen to twenty-four inches."

I still feel a pit in my stomach when a snowstorm is forecast. This feeling came from being the production manager, driver, plower, shoveler, dispatcher, and "anything that was needed" type of owner.

In the past, I would have scrambled to get the trucks ready and the equipment working. I would have called the workers and subs, started the paperwork for the work orders, shuffled the personnel, and waited to see what type of storm it was. I would have put together a schedule that worked with my resources at that time.

My command-and-control tactics required me to be in the middle of every last detail. I had to be up all hours in a nor'easter.

A two-day, two-foot storm would be one hell of an undertaking.

Julio interrupted my dread-filled daydream with the rest of his request: "Dom, I have scheduled a meeting with all the head honchos in a couple of minutes. Would you like to join us?"

We were not that same mom-and-pop business anymore, and I was not the same owner who had to manage every last detail. Now, as the leader of a $15 million property management and snow organization, snow events excited me.

I shook off that gut feeling and smiled. "Julio, I need to pour myself a cup of coffee, and then I will meet you in the conference room."

When I arrived, the room was bustling. There was a rush, an excitement in the air.

I looked around the table at everyone organizing their paperwork:

- Della, the vendor manager, was managing her lists of vendors and work orders for her subcontractors.

- Mina, the liaison manager, had piles of work orders, schedules, and snow packets for each snow team.

- Julio, the snow production manager and dispatcher, had his folder filled with schedules, workers, and equipment lists.

- Each of the six supervisors was checking with their teams, readying to cover four states.

- Mick was in charge of the equipment and trucks. He kept his laptop open and ready for any potential questions.

- Even my partner, Joseph, decided to join us. Although he wasn't part of the snow division, he was an owner, nonetheless.

Before my coffee had cooled, my right hand, Mina, leaned over and asked me teasingly, "Do you need to be here? I know you, Dom. You love to look at the systems and try to update them. We will be at battle stations for a few days, so don't get any ideas! Don't you have something else to do?"

Everyone looked at Mina and said, *"Did you say that? Now we know you must be Dom's favorite."*

Julio started the meeting.

Mina shuffled her paperwork and said, "Hey, Julio, are there any changes to the drivers, workers, or subs?"

"Yes, two drivers need to be changed—one subcontractor and these other men need to be on different crews on route three and one on route eight. I have two replacement drivers in place."

Mina said, "I will update the schedule sheets and the work orders. By tomorrow, I will have the two-day schedules and two-day work orders ready."

Julio thanked her. "Hey, Mick, any changes or issues with the trucks or equipment?"

Mick replied, "Trucks twelve and eighteen are out of service. I have truck numbers two and four to replace them during this storm. All equipment will be ready by Thursday. I have the repair department and workers scheduled with twelve-hour shifts to cover the two days."

Julio thanked Mick and then turned back to Mina. "Mina, can you make these changes too?"

Mina confirmed, "Already on it."

Della added, "I am all set with the subcontractor changes. Julio, I will have the paperwork in your hands by Thursday. All the changes with the lists will be ready for you by tomorrow."

The banter went on for just under an hour. Back and forth, everyone contributed their issues, solutions, and input. Everyone had each other's backs. I knew no one felt any of the dread I used to feel during significant events or our teams used to feel at even the mention of more work.

There was something creative going on in this room.

Something came to my mind:

This was art.

Introduction

"Leading is a skill, not a gift. You're not born with it; you learn how. "

—Seth Godin

Have you ever wondered how the business owners you admire became successful? What do they know that you need to know? How long did it take them to grow their businesses?

What did they do?

Was it luck? Was it determination?

Was it building *systems* (ah, that word we constantly hear)?

Was it becoming a *leader* (another f-ing word we constantly hear)?

You may have worked with consultants. After they help you implement a system or two, do you get this odd feeling that they must have some *secret* about how it all works together? Something they're keeping from you?

A secret that you *must* figure out?

All the books, consultants, theories, and systems out there may make sense, but they're not helpful if you can't utilize them—if you can't put all the pieces of the business puzzle together to improve your life and business.

By the way, nobody—and I mean nobody—runs a business without having the smarts to do it. You have taken risks and made sacrifices, both monetarily and emotionally. You help people and their families by creating jobs and opportunities, and in doing so, you also support the community. I am proud to be one of those entrepreneurs who creates opportunities. I am also proud of and respect the entrepreneurs who run and grow their businesses.

I'm sure you could talk to me for hours about the problems your business is facing. You've probably found a dozen reasonable solutions for each, so you must wonder why these solutions aren't working.

I understand how you feel because I've been in your shoes, working in my business, growing, becoming overwhelmed, and not knowing what to do or where to go.

I did figure out the "secret." I understood how all the pieces of the business puzzle worked together.

I made it to the light at the end of the tunnel, and it wasn't because I kept my head down until I hit some magic revenue goal, worked harder, attended the next big conference, or suddenly got smarter.

The secret to making all the pieces of the business puzzle work—the secret that it seemed like every other consultant and leadership guru was keeping from me—was that I had to transform.

The secret was me.

I don't mean me as in Business Coach Domenic or Teaching Domenic.

I mean me, as in Worker-Owner Domenic or Learning Domenic. I am the one who works 24/7, the one who wants to make it all work but cannot understand how all the pieces work together.

This Worker-Owner, Domenic, was right where I was back then.

I kept working hard, and I kept learning and growing.

Yet I found that our processes, systems, or consultant changes helped in the short run but did not help consistently later.

I had to see business in a new way. It was me!

I remember struggling (when wasn't I?) with growing my company and finding my place in the organization. I was transitioning from worker-owner to leader, but I wasn't sure where I was in the early stages of leadership development. I picked up Seth Godin's Linchpin. This book helped me see myself as the linchpin of this growth, or was I the barrier to growth and prosperity?

We were a good company, but the business was limited to what the owners could facilitate. We could hire the right people and find the best systems. We could even grow to a point. However, something would always be missing until I became a leader who could release control, mentor instead of micromanage, trust my people, and have systems run the business—all (I'm going to say it. Here it goes:) *without me*.

No matter how many times a consultant gave me the "take two systems and call me in the morning" treatment, nothing changed for the better until I became the leader I needed to be.

Watch for the tomato symbol throughout the book. These little morsels will show you key concepts, just as ripe, juicy tomatoes make the best-tasting sauce.

Look for the hummingbird symbol, which indicates other relatable moments in my Learning Domenic journey that you may find familiar.

A Quick Summary of What's to Come

Before we dig in here, please do me a favor: pick your Bullshit Card back up off the table.

I know some of you have already thrown it, and others are getting ready to.

I don't blame you.

You've heard too many leadership gurus tell you to do things just like they did, and all will be well. They can't often tell you how they did those things, really, or what it would look like in your situation.

You've also heard Simon Sinek tell us that everyone has a why, but we all know that naming your why doesn't just translate to making more money in the way some people act like it does.

You might be curious about what leadership skills you might need to improve, but I bet you have only so much patience for leadership nonsense.

So first, thank you for picking up this book (and your Bullshit Card).

Second, the story in the preface was real. I did not make it up. It wasn't a story "loosely based on actual events." It was the event. The snowstorm was one of the biggest and lasted the week. The meeting went just like that. It was one of the most profitable snowstorms we've ever had.

I imagine you'd like to have more meetings like that one. You'd like your company to have this type of employee and team strength while you sit and admire.

No one wants to read another leadership book.

As long as you feel something is missing in your business, you keep reading those books, wading through the bullshit until something catches your eye.

You don't have to believe me yet. But you can trust Annunziatina's guidance, methods, and recipes.

I know how to transform businesses into art. All the great business leaders know how to make art.

What do the great leaders and I know? We know the three key principles and how all the pieces of the business puzzle work.

First, thriving businesses are system-run organizations. Each department has its own systems, and more systems connect those departments. The people who work in those departments have templates and flows to follow within the systems. It is a *machine*. **With Ingredients 7 and 8, we'll explore the what, why, and how of this system development step.**

Second, in this thriving environment, each employee has one position, is responsible for one result, and has one responsibility to the company. From those roles, they can all work collaboratively to serve their clients. You will not see people wearing many different job titles—the proverbial wearing many different hats. You won't see people waiting for the big boss to tell them what to do or how they want it done. **That's where we'll focus our time on employee development in Ingredients 4, 5, and 6.**

Third (I'm getting very excited here), the whole company—every person—has this special *something* inside them. It's in the way they live, breathe, and operate. They seem driven by a beautiful, living force toward a shared purpose—one vision an owner and leader lead them toward. **That shared purpose is where we'll start with Ingredients 1, 2, and 3, the key of all keys, *Capo di Tutti Capi*, leader development.**

I know. "Domenic, why are you explaining the ingredients backward? Can't I skip to the last chapters, flip to the end of the book, and get to the good stuff?"

Here is why I explained this backward: Systems run the business, employees run the systems, and leaders lead the employees.

Systems run the business. They are the foundation, and they run the show. Yet, with great, professional, career-minded employees to run the systems, systems will consistently work. Lastly, all great organizations have leaders who lead the employees with vision, strategy, and mentoring.

This is where we start in Ingredient 1. It all begins with you. Remember, you're the linchpin, the rock, and the foundation of your business. The strongest leaders build and sustain the best empires.

Some Say To-may-to, Some Say To-mah-to

I told you there was a secret to why and what with all the pieces of the business puzzle; there is also a secret ingredient in Annunziatina's recipe.

The secret ingredient Annunziatina firmly has in place is love, which makes her tomato paste incredible and completes the pieces of the puzzle that make up the life she has created.

At this moment, I can*not* tell you exactly how you can create financial and professional success for everyone in your organization. However, I will tell you that when you firmly establish these three key principles (and you will), the secret ingredient will be the final piece of the business puzzle.

That is why I am starting with the first step: leadership development.

If you want to build a successful business, you need the mindset of a thriving business owner—one who's not a worker-manager.

When Annunziatina takes her three steps and combines all the ingredients in her tomato paste recipe, she creates the best tomato paste on earth, year after year.

Combining the three key principles of leadership, employee, and system development with all the ingredients in my Tomato Paste Leadership will ultimately achieve the most business success in your life.

This book's three steps mirror the key principles I teach in person and online.

The ingredients are divided into chapters that explain everything you need to know to complete those steps.

The business will sustain itself and grow when the owner has a system-oriented, mentoring, and strategy position instead of a micromanaging, just get-it-done, owner-working position. Whether teaching or sitting on the beach reading a good book and enjoying a cool beverage (this is what I do best), your teams of great people need you to lead the company while they manage the systems.

The exciting part is that I will leave you with more than the why and the what; I will not leave you to figure out the how on your own. I will give you a map and a strategy to help you put all the pieces of the business puzzle together—to jar up the tomato paste, if you will. I will be your guide through the whole process.

I love being the guide, the teacher. As a twenty-seven-year business owner and coach for the last fifteen years, that has always been the best part of my work. I also love my mother-in-law's example of teaching and passing down generational recipes and stories to her family.

If that's what you've been looking for, keep reading.

We will start with you, the leader, growing in a specific direction.

STEP 1:
Developing the Leader in You

"There are two ways to build a career or a business. We can go through life hunting and pecking, looking for opportunities or customers, hoping that something connects. Or we can go through life with intention, knowing what our piece looks like, knowing our WHY, and going straight to the places we fit."

—Simon Sinek, David Mead, and Peter Docker *Find Your Why*

You are integral to your business' growth.

Growing your company begins by nurturing the leader within yourself. These initial steps will transform you from a micro-managing owner who rules and controls everything, working 24/7, to a collaborative leader who recognizes that success hinges on the synergy between you and your dedicated team of employees.

This section will share my experiences and stories of becoming a leader. My hope is that you can relate to yourself and the trials and tribulations of your journey. The *how* is a real-life, repeatedly proven method that is simple to understand.

In fact, after reading this section, you will say, "Domenic, I knew this."

Of course you did. You wouldn't be where you are in your business if you didn't.

However, implementation is always more complex than learning. This implementation will be a lifelong journey with no quick fixes, just better choices.

The Recipe for Tomato Paste Leadership

My story starts with the scramble to survive business ownership. It continued through everything I learned to lead my company to the top 3 percent of our industry until I finally made the leap to teaching, mentoring, speaking, hosting workshops, and coaching numerous organizations. Since then, I have guided hundreds of business owners, teaching them to become mentors and leaders. I have trained their employees to think and act like owners and helped their companies build and implement streamlined systems.

During my years as a coach to young entrepreneurs, I have not given up getting coaching where I need improvement. (The old put my mouth where my money is mentality.) I have refined my coaching abilities by enhancing my speaking skills (thanks to Michael Port), developing better workshop programs (with insights from Callan Rush), mastering digital marketing (under the guidance of James Wedmore), and honing my writing and storytelling skills (inspired by Seth Godin).

My ultimate goal has always been to serve better those who are looking to grow their companies around their lives.

As I spoke and blogged more about leadership, systems, and business strategies, I noticed an interesting trend: people became more engaged when I intertwined these topics with stories of my Italian culture. I added pictures of my garden and recipes from my beloved mother-in-law to my blog. At speaking events, I began giving away fresh olive oil from my friend and client, George Trevis, who owns a vineyard, olive orchard, and B&B in Italy. He was one of my first clients. (It was hard trying to coach him via Zoom pre-covid. I just had to visit him more!!! The travesty!!!!)

Then, almost as an off-hand comment, I wrote a series about "tomato paste leadership."

Unsurprisingly, people were drawn to stories about making the best cavatelli, fettuccine, crespelle, Italian wine cookies, and tomato paste. Who wouldn't be? Readers were captivated when I shared these family traditions and our love for Italian cooking. I enjoy pairing these cultural stories with business strategies to create an engaging and relatable narrative. Both my audience and I enjoyed this blend of life and business.

Initially, I was surprised by how much Tomato Paste Leadership resonated with people. It was a straightforward metaphor for discussing exceptional processes that lead to remarkable results, whether making tomato paste or building a successful business.

Upon further reflection, I realized the depth of the metaphor. It involved selecting the right tomatoes, systematizing the canning process, teaching the next generation, and patiently crafting Mamma Annunziatina's tomato paste.

These steps paralleled the meticulous processes needed to cultivate a thriving business. You need the right employees, systemization of the business process, education programs, and leaders with vision and strategy to ensure your business thrives.

Sharing my culture, family, and history resonated with people because they longed for a deeper connection. I found from my coaching organization that people were tired of feeling trapped in a business that ran them. This is a recipe for something greater.

Systems, people, and leadership only function cohesively if the leader is willing, prepared, and knowledgeable about how to make it happen.

With enough time, I could have discovered the secret of the special sauce and made the transition independently. You can figure it out with time.

With three daughters to raise and a life I didn't want to miss out on, I chose the quicker path.

With mentoring and an "I is an engineer" mentality, Learning Domenic achieved a faster transformation:

- From a worker-owner doing everything to a mentor and visionary leader creating opportunities.

- From pushing and pulling employees unaware of the company's direction to empowering them with a clear vision of the future and their role.

- From my partner and I being the only ones thriving financially to creating a community-minded, thriving environment organization where everyone benefited.

- From a revolving door of employees to nurturing career-minded professionals who grew and prospered with owner-like dedication.

- From relying on people to wear many hats to establishing processes that allowed individuals to run the company's systems efficiently.

Now, as Teaching Domenic, I am passionate about coaching others through their transformative journeys.

What are you seeking? Are you looking to reach the next level or find a way out of the cycle of overworking for underwhelming results? Do you believe others have something you lack, or are you ready to become the leader you aspire to be?

I wrote this book to guide you back to the basics.

I understand if you're saying, "Domenic, I want results—the magic pill, the immediate transformation. Just give me the facts!"

I assure you that the basics will provide you with the knowledge you seek. There are no fancy guarantees, no pie-in-the-sky bullshit, and no unrealistic promises.

More than just the facts.

Ask any business owner who has transitioned from good to great, "What did you do? How did you do it?"

They will agree it comes down to three key principles:

1. Establish consistent systems that lead to predictable results.

2. Create an environment where employees can thrive and grow.

3. Develop yourself as a leader.

Were you seeking just the facts? It is that simple! You don't need more information than that.

Now, the secret sauce: You need a plan of action and a method for implementing what you already know. It's essential to understand how all the pieces of the business puzzle fit together.

Additionally, it would be best to connect everything to a more profound sense of meaning—your why, your purpose, what you want to become, and how you want to live. That's where our recipe begins.

To learn more about how Tomato Paste and Tomato Paste Leadership, click here or put the link in your browser for bonus material on my website: TomatoPasteLeadership.com/bonus.

INGREDIENT 1:
Purpose in Life

"We must not get so wrapped up in our work that we think we're immune from the reality of aging and life. Who wants to be the person who can never let go? Is there so little meaning in your life that your only pursuit is work until you're eventually carted off in a coffin? Take pride in your work. But it is not all."

—Ryan Holiday and Stephen Hanselman,
The Daily Stoic

You want to grow your company.

What does it take to be the leader of this growing company—a company that is meaningful to the client, the employees, the community, your family, and you?

More importantly, *why* do you want to grow your company?

Have you ever asked yourself these questions?

As a coach, I can sense the excitement of the owners and employees when I am in a new organization. Deep down, I may have a mean streak because I like to dampen that energy with this first question. It always seems to stump them.

Why do you want to grow?

Chirp, chirp, chirp, go the crickets.

Tilt goes the head, like a puppy unsure what it hears.

The truth is, there are many reasons a person might want to grow their business:

- To have the freedom to live and work the way you want.
- To create a business that mirrors your values and culture.
- To be a leader in your industry.
- To know that your family and community are proud of you.
- To make a difference.
- To have more financial abundance for your family.

I always want to have success in the truest sense of the word.

When I ask this question outright, some owners don't know how to answer it.

Few people stop considering why they want to grow, apart from "To make more money." Once you're five or ten years in, you think growth is a given—that you *should* want to make more money.

The problem is there's more to growth than making a profit.

If an owner cannot tell me why they want to grow, how the hell can we build a strategy or set up systems based on those values?

If you don't make choices based on what is important to you and don't know where you're going, who knows where you will end up?

Your business strategy starts *not* with the business but with your life.

How does one start with life?

The easy answer is to clarify your Purpose in Life. Again, this is an easy answer yet a bit more complex to implement. This linchpin answer helps you better understand what you believe in, where you are going, and how to make the best choices to get there.

We're going to get serious here.

You are about to learn what happens when you have your why.

I, too, learned what happened when I did this exercise for myself, down to a bullet-point level. My strategy coach taught me that when I was at any crossroads in life, I needed to be able to refer back to that purpose. I needed to know exactly where I would devote my energy anytime, anywhere. It was a way to reflect on how I was living and leading.

It was a way to realize what it would take to become successful, *including what I defined success as* creating a thriving organization in the top three percent.

Key Concepts: Purpose in Life.

Resounding Success: There is a more resounding and meaningful form of success to pursue beyond financial status, power, and material possessions. Success is what truly matters to you.

Personal Values: Your Purpose in Life are the values you believe in and live by. You have deeply held convictions that are unique to you. Exploring and living your Purpose leads to a greater sense of purpose and direction.

Freedom from External Standards: Your Purpose in Life is not about right or wrong; they are not things you will only state and then forget. Your Purpose in Life is hugely personal and unique to you. Trust your inner wisdom, and follow your path toward them.

Understanding and Alignment: You can use Purpose in Life to have what you want and eliminate what you don't want in your life and what keeps you from living your dreams and values. This enables alignment between actions and values.

Empowered Decision-Making: Making better choices gives you the energy, enthusiasm, and commitment to live what is important to you. It allows you to transform and be motivated to make positive changes.

CHAPTER 1:
Grow in the Right Direction

"If you want to be a leader who attracts quality people, the key is to become a person of quality yourself."

—Jim Rohn

I didn't start out dreaming of being a business owner. To quote my dad, "I is an engineer."

I followed in his footsteps first when I received a bachelor's degree in computer engineering from my dad's alma mater, UConn, and again when I interned for six years under him in his electronics manufacturing business. I immediately became a partner, and for five years, we built our business into a multimillion-dollar enterprise. When Dad was ready to become more of a sage and mentor and less of a business owner, we sold it, and I partnered in a landscaping/snow removal business.

We were two hardworking Italian boys working 24/7, full of piss and vinegar, and making a damn good living. We grew the business inch by inch for ten years and were happy to do whatever it took to make things run.

It took us ten exciting years to nearly double the business' sales from $400,000 to $700,000. The profits afforded each of us an excellent salary, just in time. When my wife and I found out our family was growing by not one, not two, but three babies, my sense of urgency to keep pushing the business further only grew.

Around the time my daughters turned four years old, my wife and I decided to take the family to Disney World.

I remember getting on my hands and knees and gathering them around me. "Girls, we have a surprise for you: we're going to Mickey's house!"

Pandemonium unleashed.

Their excitement was unreal. Mine was, too—you can't beat those smiles in the moments burned in my mind.

Of course, in the back of my head, a little voice wasn't so happy.

I had heard that voice so many times before. Whenever I decided between working and being at home or part of the family, that voice constantly nagged me, "Work is first."

This time, that nagging little voice was going to be quiet. I wanted to spend as much free time as possible with my girls and enjoy my family.

Guess what. The work got done anyway.

Before leaving for Disney, I did everything possible to ensure my employees were set up for the week. After all, the work still needed to be done, and since I thought I was a big-time business owner back then, the preparation was quite the undertaking.

When I look back on how I ran my company, I can see that I was a "command and control" owner. I controlled all aspects of my business.

I picked up my phone whenever it rang.

I made the schedule.

I helped load the trucks to get the crews out on time.

I had my truck and crew to load up.

I drove.

I dug the holes.

I checked on everyone else when I had time to leave my crew and work.

I spoke to the clients.

Did estimates.

Solved issues.

Ordered materials.

On and on and on.

After a twelve-hour day, I would try to enjoy dinner with my wife and three baby daughters. Still sad but true, my mind was on work. So, right after putting my daughters to bed, I went straight to my bedroom office to finish the day's paperwork.

The payroll had to be posted.

The crew information had to be transmitted to my partner.

The vendor vouchers had to be checked and posted.

That was my everyday life.

Sound familiar?

I knew I could have a great vacation if I got all my ducks in a row. Of course, getting my ducks in a row meant setting up all the crews and the office to run those tasks without me. But that was what I did. I went into each "department" of the company and set up every aspect, every employee, and every detail to run smoothly while we set off for Mickey's house.

What Matters to You?

Sure, profit matters. Systems matter. But no system in the world will help you get what you want if you don't know what you want. So, as we set off on our tomato paste journey together, I'm going to ask you the same question that I ask every single business owner who asks me how to grow their company:

Why?

Why do you want to grow your business?

We all know that a business is supposed to have a purpose and a good reason for being, but as soon as we run the company, it becomes all about growth and profits. We strive for more revenue, clients, work, teams, and systems...until suddenly, we find our whole life is the business.

We're so used to thinking of growing profits as the marker of a good business that we forget that a good business is what makes profits grow.

Early on, I thought I had a good business, but I had to be there every second of the day—to keep our patched-together systems running and ensure the people knew what they were doing.

I had to be there because the business wouldn't be a business if I weren't.

I also had to be there because being there made me feel like somebody.

Years later, it wasn't until I learned what it was to be a leader that my focus changed. I figured out that my business was there to work for us—not just me and my family but the people I hired and their families and lives. I stopped worrying about growing profits and started focusing on developing my people. Incidentally, focusing on my employees (don't think I wasn't thinking about the finances. Hey, I'm a businessman.) created the business growth explosion.

Every one of my companies that grew to a multimillion-dollar level...

Every single company that I coached to a multimillion-dollar level...

Every business associate I have masterminded as they led a multimillion-dollar organization...

Without exception, every success story follows the three key principles I named earlier:

- Establish systems that lead to predictable results.

- Create an environment where employees can thrive and grow.

- Develop yourself as a leader.

That's what this book is all about.

My why for running and growing my landscaping/snow removal business was deeply rooted in my desire to provide for my wife and daughters. However, as you'll discover in the upcoming pages, they quickly helped me realize how far I had strayed from my original purpose. It took me some time to come to terms with this revelation and determine what steps to take next. In the following chapters, I'll take you on my journey from that gut-wrenching realization to how I took action.

CHAPTER 2:
Tomorrowland

"Your vision will become clear only when you look into your heart. Who looks outside, dreams. Who looks inside, awakes."

—Carl Jung

My daughters held tight to our hands, dragging me, my wife, my parents, and my favorite mom-in-law from one side of the park to the other.

We were having a blast.

"Daddy, Daddy! Small World!"

"Daddy, Daddy! Peter Pan!"

"Daddy, Daddy! Teacups!"

Even those f-ing nauseating teacups are a blast when your kids are enjoying them.

Then we arrived in Tomorrowland—their first roller coaster ride. (Yes, I'm talking about the PeopleMover. Can you imagine me telling my daughters we had to hold our hands up going around corners just like you see on TV? I did! We fathers can exaggerate a lot for kids at that age.)

As we came off the "roller coaster," my phone rang.

I took it with a flip of the cell phone without a second thought. I handled the crisis while holding my little daughter, Toni, by the hand. My wife and parents looked on with what I thought was admiration.

This wasn't my first call of the day. That phone was power. I was one of the big boys in the industry. I was running my ship.

I had life by the balls. I was important. I was somebody. Hear me roar.

I couldn't see myself through my family's eyes. I couldn't see what I had become.

I thought that was how an owner acted. No matter when they came in, taking calls was evidence of my importance. Wasn't being a leader about freedom to work from anywhere?

I look back and think, *What an idiot.* I could have been home for supper, a wedding, or a funeral! I still answered that phone, period.

I have always seen this behavior at conferences and still see it when I speak on stage. I am in the middle of showing them how to become better leaders and build solid systems, and people get up to take that "one" call. In and out they go. I am not knocking them; I was that person.

It looks silly to me now, but my girls saw through it all even before they were tall enough for the real roller coasters.

Before I had resolved whatever crisis was on the other line, Toni started to tug at my hand. When I looked down, she said, "Daddy, look around! We're in Tomorrowland. When are you going to stop working?"

Then my daughter Rachael pulled at my pants and said, "Daddy, Daddy, please get off the phone."

I told them both that I wasn't really working and that it was *just one call.*

Then Jessica flew over and landed right before me like a ninja. She planted two feet, put her hands up to stop the presses, and said, "No, Daddy. You are on the phone all the time."

Holy shit! Time stopped.

Everything stopped except the sweat trickling down my back.

I was stunned.

I muttered something or other to the supervisor on the other end, ended the call, and stared at my girls.

Then I looked around for support.

Favorite mother-in-law? Not a word.

Wife? Nothing.

Dad? Nothing.

You would think my mom would help me, but she just shook her head with the "I love you anyway" look that moms give.

Now I know why God gave me triplets: I'm so thick-headed that I needed to hear the message three times.

They were right, and it hit me like a ton of bricks.

I was not a big-time businessman. I was on the phone at Mickey's house for crying out loud.

As my daughters' words echoed, a flood of emotions washed over me. I was surrounded by Tomorrowland's magic yet utterly disconnected from these beautiful family moments.

In that instant, I saw myself through my daughters' eyes, but not as the powerful businessman I had imagined. Their innocence revealed the simple truth: I had become so consumed by work that I had lost sight of what truly mattered and what I cherished most: time with them.

My Journey Begins

Whether your awakening was as vibrant and visceral as mine—filled with lights, colors, sounds, cut-with-a-knife humidity, and a touch of teacup-induced nausea—I believe you can understand the struggle of losing yourself in pursuing success.

It's all too easy to equate being busy with productivity and growth. I fell right into that trap when I forgot that work should only be a part of my life, not the entirety.

I was not the big-time business owner I thought I was.

My daughters wanted *me*. They craved my attention. My focus. My time.

What I thought I was giving my daughters and my family was not what they wanted or needed. It wasn't what I needed either. They deserved my attention, focus, and time. What I had to learn is that I deserved them too.

I deserved to live the life I was building instead of just sacrificing for it all the time.

I wanted to grow a thriving company and provide more for my family, but I now knew that hard work alone wasn't enough.

I am sure you can relate to starting with boundless energy and noble intentions. Maybe you only found yourself at a crossroads when reality set in.

Despite your most significant efforts, your business demands even more of you while yielding less for your business or life.

What next? Do you scale back and settle for less, or push forward, hoping not to lose sight of the beauty you've created?

I yearned to build a great company for my family and me to be proud of. But at what expense?

I remember thinking, "How can I work *so hard and still not give my family what they need?*"

What do I do now that my business has taken over my time and life?

What happens when hard work just isn't enough to fix the problems anymore?

Surrounded by the energy and excitement of Magic Kingdom, with my daughters by my side, I had a moment of clarity. I realized that success couldn't just be about financial achievements. Something was missing. It had to include the things that truly matter to me—being present, connected, and living a life of balance.

At that moment, as I watched my daughters, I promised myself that I would prioritize what mattered most and ensure that work would no longer overshadow the joy of family and the richness of life.

Now, I had absolutely no idea *how* to change my business or myself, yet I was at a crossroads in life. I felt determined—mindlessly, of course, but determined—to make that change.

With that decision, a new chapter of my journey began—one of rediscovery, growth, and the pursuit of true fulfillment.

Discovering My Purpose in Life.

My life before Tomorrowland had been enriched with invaluable lessons from the outstanding mentorship of my dad, family, education, experience, and Italian heritage. Growing up, I was instilled with values that guided me to get that far:

- **God** was a pillar of strength and guidance in my life, grounding me in times of uncertainty.

- **Hard work** wasn't just a concept but a way of life. My grandparents' mantra, "Work hard, and if that doesn't work, work harder," became the driving force behind every endeavor.

- **Family** was the heartbeat of everything. From lively dinner-table discussions to shared laughter and love, our bond was unbreakable.

- **Good food** brought it all together. Ah, the joys of Italian cuisine—a celebration of life, love, and togetherness. Our gatherings were filled with the aroma of home-made pasta and discussions around the table. Some would say these were loud discussions, but they don't know what loud is.

My business-owner dad was my first true mentor. He gave me a lifetime of experience in those first years of interning. Every day after school, from high school to college, I was there at his electronic company, learning how to run a business, even if it was through one of my weekly duties: cleaning the bathrooms.

He learned from my grandparents, who didn't have two nickels to rub together when they came to this country to make a better life for the family. They taught him to provide for his family 24/7, especially as the man of the house. Society may have changed in that sense, with two having to provide, but somebody always has to provide. When the time came for me to start a family, that provider sense was part of me, and I loved it.

I thought I was living up to my grandparents in a way that would make my family proud—until that moment of awakening in Tomorrowland changed everything.

Reflecting on my journey, I realize that while I had some pieces of the puzzle for business success, I needed to include critical elements of the life I truly desired. Plenty of pieces were handed down by my grandparents' work ethic, my parents' family values, my wife's unwavering support, and my daughters' eye-opening honesty. Don't get me wrong. Those were *good* pieces. My grandparents gave me a drive to work hard. My mom gave me a strong family culture. My dad gave me knowledge from his experience being a father and running a company. My wife gave me love and support.

Then, my daughters started something in me that day in Tomorrowland. In one moment, their words set me on a transformative path. Later, I discovered it was a path from worker-owner to leader with a vision for something greater than mere growth—a vision for genuine purpose.

What did this vision for genuine purpose even mean? What did it look like? I needed those missing pieces to wrestle with questions that had no clear answers.

Today, I understand that greatness isn't a one-size-fits-all concept. It's about defining success on our terms and charting a course that aligns with our values and aspirations.

The first step toward that vision is naming your Purpose in Life, clarifying your purpose, and paving the way for life and business to be filled with meaning and fulfillment.

CHAPTER 3:
Your Purpose in Life

"Greatness is primarily not a function of circumstance. Greatness, it turns out, is primarily a matter of conscious choice and discipline."

—Jim Collins, *Good to Great*

I thought I knew what I wanted. I wanted to transform my business and create a thriving organization. I wanted a higher income, happiness, better working systems, and better employees.

I found myself consumed with all these things I wanted, wanted, wanted.

When you want to grow your business and feel the success you create, you have to pause to reflect on why you want to grow. To do that, you must ask, "How do I envision my life?"

Sure, implementing streamlined systems, hiring exceptional employees, and being the best leader are the keys to greater success. I do not doubt this. But looking back from my Teaching Domenic's perch, I realize that the steps *before* creating the systems, hiring the best employees, and transforming all lie within you.

True satisfaction requires more than mere desires—it demands a clear vision and alignment with your deepest values.

Your why.

Your vision.

Your values.

Your Purpose in Life.

I encountered the concept of Purpose in Life from my dad and from reading the greats: Michael Gerber's *The E-Myth,* Simon Sinek's book *Start with Why,* Napoleon Hill's *Think and Grow Rich,* and Dale Carnegie's *How to Win Friends and Influence People.* These and many other books about your why and purpose deepened my journey of being a leader in life and business.

Your Purpose in Life captures a broad and profound scope—it's not just about a single reason or focus but encompasses the entirety of your life's direction and meaning.

Whatever you call the innermost motivating strength that drives you, it is the foundational step that powers your growth. It is your direction and purpose.

Identifying my Purpose in Life helped ground me in my personal life and business as a leader. It helped me make life decisions with a solid understanding of what is and is not important to me. I also coach my clients to uncover these as they identify what is and is not important to them.

Successful Entrepreneurs Start Here

Not long ago, I worked with a client. Let's call him Stefano. He was at a crossroads in life.

Lucky for us both, he had a large whiteboard to work on.

He wrote what he wanted from life on one side of the board. What did he love? What made him the happiest? He wrote a lot about his family, his faith, his parents, his friends, his legacy, and his career.

On the other side of the board, we wrote, "What do you hate?" He wrote about how his boss treated him, his lack of time, stress, health, and inability to build a business as he wanted.

This work took five sessions over two months with him.

Once Stefano found his top five purposes, I asked him about his number-one purpose: family. He said his family gave him the most satisfaction and strength. When he valued it from one to ten, he said, "I would make it twenty if I could."

I said, "Great. Okay, let's look at your last month, maybe three months. How did you live that value?"

We looked closely. I asked him, "How much time did you spend with your family? How many times did you go away? Did you do things with them? Did you teach them? Did you travel with them? Did you go to church with them? What did you do?"

He said, "Well, I did my best. I would give it an eight."

His beautiful wife was there, too. She said lovingly, as only a caring wife could, "You were not here. Even when you were home, you were making client calls. I know you mean well, but Stefano, let's be honest."

How he lived out the value of family came down to a four.

Next, I pointed to the board and said, "One of the things you hate is spending all your time in the business—from one to ten; how much do you hate it?"

Ten.

"How much did you live it anyway?"

Ten.

It can be shocking to see where you're living.

When I struggled with this in my business, my dad told me, "Life is like a dark room. You cannot see anything in the room until you turn the light switch on. After that, no matter what you do—you can turn the light switch on or off—you will always know what is in the room." Once my daughters turned the light on for me to see that I was in the wrong place, I couldn't unseen what was in that room. But I could make better decisions. I could make it right.

When we laid it out on his whiteboard, Stefano realized that he was living in his pain and fears rather than what he wanted out of life. It had been easier for him to live on his "do not want" list than to overcome his barriers. At least it had been easier before he turned on the light and saw what he had been doing.

How to Name Your Purpose in Life

In your journey to uncover your Purpose in Life, you may find it beneficial to draw upon various resources that offer guidance and insight into personal development. I have found books, especially audiobooks, to be one of the best sources of help. These audiobooks are like a coach in a box. I turned to audiobooks when I needed help learning a business or life concept. The books appeared when I needed them. While I listened to the brilliant authors, they spoke to and coached me directly. To this day, I still listen and learn from audiobooks for my continuing personal development.

Learning has always been at the core of who I am—not just for the sake of knowing but to grow. Over the years, I've absorbed ideas from many coaches, hundreds of books, programs, and workshops, reworked them, and integrated them into my coaching approach. I believe that knowledge only becomes powerful when it is implemented. For me, it's not about being smarter; it's about becoming a better coach, mentor, and leader. The lessons from these coaches, books, and courses have shaped me and strengthened my ability to teach, inspire, and empower others, creating lasting impact in their lives and businesses.

A common thread in these leadership books is that one's *Purpose in Life* is the foundation of all success in life and business. By starting with your purpose in life, I've helped many clients discover their 'why' and build businesses that truly support their lives. This approach has proven to be a better way to serve my clients, guiding them to create businesses that align with their deeper purpose.

In a nutshell, you'll begin by listing what you want and do not want in life. Then, you'll prioritize those lists to identify your Purpose in Life and determine what to measure your investment of time and energy against. Once your Purpose in Life feels final, you will identify what keeps you from living it out.

Let's be clear: you do not *create* your Purpose in Life. This isn't about discovering something new. Your Purpose in Life is what's already inside you.

This journey starts with what you deeply believe in. Your Purpose in Life will become your map. It is easy to say, "I *believe* this," or "I *don't believe* that," but I am asking you to write about what is essential. It takes a bit more thinking to write something out and make it sense than to say something that sounds good.

When contemplating whether to sell my partnerships in 2011 or continue leading them, I turned to the Purpose in Life. I wrote down in 1996 after my daughters helped me find my purpose in Tomorrowland. I know that this tool helped me make the best decision. My partner and I were at a crossroads with the strategic direction of our businesses. Because I look at my Purpose in Life yearly to assess how I am living and how my success is going, this assessment helped me look at what is important to me and what is not, whether or not I am living my Purpose in Life, and what is in the way. Like any map, sometimes you take a wrong turn, yet you can stop, breathe, ask for help, reroute, and start again. That is the beauty of naming your Purpose in Life. Today, when I assess my Purpose in Life, I see that my choices and paths led me to the right destination.

Having a written foundation for a life plan and understanding what motivates you is essential. But where you invest your time, money, and energy matters.

How are you living out your strategy in your everyday choices? Where do you put your resources? How much room does your business take up in your life, and how much do you want it to?

Self-awareness is like flipping on a light in a dark room—you can't navigate without seeing where you are. Begin by reflecting on what truly fulfills and motivates you. This clarity helps bridge the gap between where you are and where you want to be. Without self-awareness, pursuing goals that don't truly serve you is easy.

Areas to Consider

I have listed some significant areas that I find meaningful. They are the basis of my and many clients' Purpose in Life. The following process will create a powerful guide for what is or is not essential in your life. Your business must work within and around your life. Reflecting on these aspects of your life will be helpful when defining your purpose in life.

These may not encompass everything, but these areas can help you focus on the key areas that matter most:

- **Family**: What do you desire in your marriage or intimate relationships? How do you see yourself as a parent or caregiver?

- **Social**: How do you want to spend time with friends, in recreation, or through travel?

- **Career/Business**: What role does your career play in your life? How do you want your business to align with your life's priorities?

- **Education/Personal Growth**: What do you want to learn—for professional development or personal enrichment?

- **Spirituality**: What are your core values in faith or spiritual growth?

- **Community**: How do you want to contribute and engage with your community?

- **Time**: Do you have the freedom to spend time on what truly matters to you?

- **Health**: How do you prioritize your physical, mental, and emotional well-being?

Define What is Important

Take a piece of paper or a whiteboard to work through these next steps. Use the areas above to help you zero in on what is essential in your life. Writing by hand connects your inner thoughts with action, helping you focus and clarify your intentions.

Ask yourself:

- What does my ideal life look and feel like?
- What do I value most deeply?
- What brings me the greatest joy and satisfaction?
- How would I spend my time if there were no constraints?
- What activities bring fulfillment to my daily life?
- What drives me to wake up and stay engaged each day?
- What legacy do I want to leave?
- How do I want to be remembered by my loved ones?

Write these thoughts down and refine them until they feel authentic and deeply personal. Take time with these questions, adding to your list as inspirations arise. Then, identify the five items that resonate most with you. These represent your core desires.

For example, when I was a partner in my landscaping business, one of my purposes in life was to grow a business where everyone could thrive professionally and financially. I learn this from working with my dad. It hasn't changed today; this value to build now is helping other business owners grow their businesses and achieve success without compromising their values.

Prioritize with Courage

Fear often prevents people from living lives aligned with their true priorities. They might fear losing control, breaking away from their comfort zone, or not meeting others' expectations. However, courage is essential for focusing on what truly matters. To take meaningful steps forward, they must first identify the barriers that keep them stuck.

Barriers often show up as things we tolerate but dislike—those aspects of life that drain our energy, erode motivation, or distract us from our purpose. Let's uncover them with a focused exercise:

Take a moment to shift your focus inward and create a list of what you don't want in your life. This might include circumstances, tasks, relationships, or habits that negatively impact your well-being. To guide your thinking, consider these questions:

- What situations leave me feeling stressed, sad, or drained?

- What responsibilities or commitments do I dread the most?

- Which daily routines or habits feel unproductive or unfulfilling?

- What environments or interactions consistently sap my energy?

- When do I feel most frustrated or dissatisfied with my choices?

- What patterns or behaviors would I like to leave behind?

- Which relationships no longer align with my values or priorities?

- What compromises have I made that no longer serve my purpose?

Once you've created your list, please review it and identify the top five items that cause the most discomfort or dissatisfaction. These are the things you no longer want to tolerate in your life. They represent the barriers that block your growth and alignment.

Why This Step Matters: Acknowledging what you don't want is often easier than articulating what you want, but both are crucial. Confronting what drains or distracts you takes a decisive step toward clarity and self-awareness. When you dare to let go of these barriers, you free up the energy and focus to prioritize what truly matters.

Prioritize Your Purpose in Life and Desires

Now that your creative juices are flowing and your lists are in hand, it's time to prioritize your top desires and purposes.

The top five things you want in life aren't equal, but it's too easy to say, "Family first." The clearer you can be about your order of Purpose in Life, the more precise you can be about your priorities.

Begin by tentatively ranking your desires from one to five based on your instincts. Then, compare each pair of desires and ask yourself which is more important. Adjust the ranking accordingly until you feel satisfied with the order.

These are your Purposes in Life. They can help you find your direction, guide your decisions, and drive you toward success. These prioritized desires form your Purpose in Life, guiding your choices and actions in life.

You may want to do the same thing for your life's "do not wants."

Assess Alignment

In the same way that you need to get clear about what matters most to you, you need to be explicit about your Purpose and how you live it. It's crucial to assess whether your actions align with your aspirations.

Now, let's go further than analyzing your ideals. You need to examine your Purpose *and* consider how you are living it. These answers require honesty.

With your Purpose in Life list of your top five purposes, assign a value ranking to each Purpose on a scale of 1–10, with 10 being the highest. Then, indicate how well you believe you currently live those values.

Example:

- How much do I *value* Purpose 1?

- How much do I *live* Purpose 1?

And so on for each Purpose.

You will be surprised by this exercise. Speaking from experience, what I value is not always what I live. To track your progress, revisit these purposes and assessments regularly— monthly, quarterly, or yearly—to identify discrepancies and reflect on what prevents you from achieving your life's Purposes or pulls you into undesirable situations.

Overcome Barriers

How we invest our resources—our time, skills, and energy—determines our life path. However, aligning your purposes and actions requires effectively managing your resources.

Sometimes, our actions align closely with our intentions. But often, we do things quite differently from our Purposes in Life. While unexpected challenges and opportunities may arise, the best route is to seek options that align with your Purpose in Life, even amid pressures. This is life.

One of your Purposes in Life will be related to your business or career. We are looking for alignment between work and life, not trying to eliminate work completely. Building my business and helping others develop it has been one of my Purpose in Life from day one—a business-related Purpose is not a barrier.

Barriers are misplaced priorities that distract us from our actual Purposes in Life and can be overcome.

Identify opportunities to prioritize what matters to you, manage your resources, and nourish your life and business in alignment with the purposes you're genuinely drawn toward.

One of the most common fears I encounter in coaching is the fear of change. Clients cling to familiar patterns because they equate control with security. However, they can find new freedom and focus by identifying the root of their fears and systematically addressing them.

At first, it might not seem like fear is part of this equation. What could be scary about doing what you want to do? But I often find that owners are attached to the feeling of control that "being an owner" gives them. They fear losing everything if they don't hold tightly enough to it all—their status, profits, or ability to know what's coming next and what they'll do when it does. There is a fear of losing the validation and satisfaction that comes from working hard, doing it all yourself, and holding all the rewards.

They're also suffering from inexperience. They don't have models teaching them how to be leaders, examples to follow, or clout offered up for being anything less than the command-and-control "big boss."

The truth is that your organization can only grow as much as you're willing to let go of control. To face your fears.

Keeping a tight grip on every aspect of your business can help you achieve a specific goal, but it will cost you.

If you're still not sure what I mean, take some time to look closely at that cost. What's your Tomorrowland moment?

Making different choices might be difficult, but I'm willing to bet it'll be worth it.

I have been coaching for some time. It always amazes me to hear my clients profess that their family is their number-one Purpose. Yet with this assessment system, they often find the Purposes in Life that are most important, and they are living at a three, four, or five. Don't get me wrong. I am not judging, only assessing. The choices are personal. I, too, was surprised when I was doing this process. I professed that my wife, daughters and family were number one. Yet I was not acting in this manner. Remember, we are building a life first and then a business that works around this life. I promise this foundation will help you become a better leader and develop your life and business in a way that satisfies your purposes.

CHAPTER 4:
Reality Check

"If you don't try to create the future you want, you must endure the future you get."

—John C. Maxwell

We all have a certain amount of time each day—a certain amount of energy.

Your business is part of that life but not your whole life.

You also have a family. It is the most important reason to want your business to grow. A family is the most significant way you experience happiness in life.

You also have personal passions: health, friendships, faith, personal development. These values give you motivation and create opportunities for you.

We all need money. You do have one of your life purposes: to run a business. You must make profit a priority. It cannot be left to chance. Money isn't evil—the *love* of money is. What a conundrum for money to both be and not be the most crucial thing to success.

Perhaps your life purpose and how you live your life seem to be at odds.

You, like Stefano, probably saw this in the last chapter's coaching session. What he valued, family, was not where he spent his time. Again, making a living and what we value the most seem to be at odds.

What do you devote your time and energy to in a given day? How much effort and time do you put into what is important to you—your family, friends, business, employees, business, and dreams?

How do you decide which deeply held purpose gets the most attention?

Allocating your time and energy resources to activities that create immediate, visible accomplishments in your business is easy. Tangible progress is rewarding.

Societal pressures may also direct your focus toward choices that show monetary results.

Show me the money.

Relationship outcomes cannot be seen as tangibly as your business accomplishments.

They don't offer the same instant gratification. (Or do they?)

They will always be there. (Are you sure?)

The truth is that what you value in theory and what you live out combine to produce the life you envision, according to your Purpose in Life.

You have some choices to make.

Making Choices

When my daughters got a little older, they joined a ballet studio. Every October, they participated in a production of *The Nutcracker.* For months, they would rehearse three nights a week and on Saturdays.

I loved to take them, and I loved to stay and watch. I loved how they started messy in the beginning moments and slowly improved to eventually perform a memorable show.

One night, when I took my daughters to the ballet studio, Rachael had something to say. Just before she started to rehearse, she told me, "Thanks for dropping us off, Dad, but you don't have to stay. I know how much work you have. We will be here for two or three hours. You should go back home to do the work."

I said, "No, honey. I love this rehearsal part as much as the actual show. I am staying. Thank you, but I want to watch you three go from the rehearsals to the final shows."

You can only imagine the smile on my daughter's face. I watched as she proudly and determinedly twirled into the rehearsal room. I still see and feel her smile.

Before Tomorrowland, I would have been tempted to leave and return to work.

Scratch that. I am *sure* I would have left.

It is not easy to break away from short-term fulfillment. But when I neglected those beautiful moments with my family, I did not see the damage I was doing in the short and long terms.

Now that the light had been turned on, I was determined to make better choices. Once I saw my purpose in life, I always looked for them and thought about them. One was (and is) growing my business, but my first three are family, health, and learning.

"A lot of work" always had to be done, but could I do that another time?

Looking back, I realize that so much of the work I thought I had to do could have been done later.

Of course, critical work needs attention. I am not out of touch or making up tall tales about how I was always there, period, no ifs, ands, or buts. You know, and I know, that the work that goes into building and leading an organization is unbelievable.

Tomato Paste Leadership is how you overcome this impossible time constraint.

With experience and coaching, I learned the difference between what was critical and what was as pressing as my daughters growing up.

The work was always going to be there—they were not.

But didn't I have to constantly grow my business? Of course I did.

Let me shout this from the rooftops: *this transformation did not happen overnight.*

It took time to learn that when I focused on my purposes and not just the tangible outcomes, better choices became available to me. When I had my Purpose in Life in place and with the proven tools that make up Tomato Paste Leadership, I built my company into an organization that gave me success in life and business.

Remember Mina's "Domenic, don't you have something else to do?"

I stopped believing that my life belonged in the office.

If I really wanted to do everything for my family, I needed to learn to grow the business in a way that would allow me to be part of that family. I needed to increase my freedom financially and managerially. I *needed* to spend more time with my family.

Rest assured that you will also uncover what is required to build your business, which works around your life.

What resources do you allocate to your Purposes in Life? Each one is equally vital to your success. One without the others will result in unhappiness in the long term.

Are you measuring your success against what you most desire? What you measure will determine what you concentrate on, so make sure you're paying attention to what you desire.

How do you decide who gets what? Your Purpose of Life will include your business and relationships, which sometimes feel at odds. Sometimes, you work more than you want, and your business growth feels slower as you tend to your health or family.

Review your Purpose in Life periodically to ensure consistency in your decision-making. Focus and intention make the difference, even when making hard choices.

What I am teaching here is not easy, but the concept is easy. Your choices will be the challenge.

Making *Better* Choices

Not long ago, at a family picnic, an old friend, Mario, and I shared business war stories over a beer and a sausage-and-pepper sandwich. One of our favorite topics, our daughters, came up. We talked about being part of their lives and what we missed in their lives. We also talked about how we sometimes used our businesses as excuses.

Our shared Italian immigrant culture had allowed us to say, "It's the company. I'm the owner. I need to be there."

Most of us can relate. A comment that stops all the trains in our family in their tracks is, "I have to work."

He said it perfectly: "Most times, it was just an excuse. All I had to say was, 'I have to work,' and boom. No issue with the spouse or family."

My friend Mario expressed some remorse in his voice when he said, "Dom, I missed out on so much. Now that I have more time, they are in college. The house is empty."

Just then, a family member joined our table. He said, "My daughter just graduated. She picked her college. She is so excited to start the new chapter in her life." He told us he had to miss his daughter's orientation. He would have needed a day off, but he couldn't possibly do that. He had to be at work.

Mario and I just looked at each other. If there ever was a Bullshit Card that needed to be thrown, it was on that table at that moment.

We were just discussing the choice between work and family. Work was the easy answer, but spending time with our family and what we worked for was the more challenging choice.

When the family member left, Mario and I discussed how this orientation moment had passed and would never happen again. How sad.

I am sure you can relate, and I am sure you can think back on something similar in your life.

What on earth makes us forget this?

Mario's most important purpose was to be part of his family. To that end, he used his business and Italian values of hard work to improve his business and create a better life.

He didn't learn soon enough what I learned in Tomorrowland—that family was more important than the business that supported them—until it was too late.

The family member who joined us was puzzled because he hadn't learned it yet. "I had to work," was his answer.

Listening to friends, family, and clients tell me what they value and seeing how they act sometimes saddens me. What are they actually choosing? I understand they see and feel short-term happiness, but I don't know if they realize they may create long-term unhappiness.

I was fortunate enough to listen to my daughters and make changes before they grew up and moved on.

You still have many years left to live. If you are looking for success in your life *and* your business, consider these chapters (ingredients). If I know one thing in my life, these ideas, methods, and processes work.

You have heard this saying: "If you think you can or if you think you can't, you are right."

Most business owners and so many people think they can't build a business *and* have a successful life. I think I can. Interestingly, we are both right.

Ballet lessons are long gone, but our memories of being there are not.

Here is what my choices did for me today.

Today, my daughters are part of my life, and they still want me to be part of theirs. When they asked us to help them move to an apartment in another country, my wife and I stopped whatever was pressing at the time. I spent time with my mother-in-law to create the garden that makes her happy, and we took ten days off to travel to Utah's national parks.

I guide them when they ask (or don't), learn to become a better teacher, help others succeed, and stay healthy.

We cannot achieve and complete our values like we can our goals. Purpose in Life is enduring. I cannot reach "the most family time ever" and move on. It can only be an ongoing focus in my life, and that only happens when I make choices that prioritize my family.

Goals may guide the short-term toward long-term success. For example, buying a car is a goal. It begins with a need. You save money, look for cars, research, get a loan, and then buy the car. This goal has a clear start and end. However, it could also be part of a larger purpose. For example, one of my long-term purposes is traveling with family and friends and buying a car, while a short-term goal contributes to fulfilling that broader, ongoing purpose of traveling.

If you are as ambitious as I am, you will work to follow your Purposes in Life. We both know that will give you a different happiness and success. We also know that the opposite will happen if you unknowingly allocate fewer and fewer resources to what you claim is most important.

When you know where you're going, you find a way there. When you keep your Purpose in Life in mind and see what you want your life to look like, you can design a strategy to make the business part of that life (without it taking over).

To build your business around your life, start this bad boy with the next ingredient: creating your Strategic Objective.

To learn more about how to create your Purpose in Life, click here or put the link in your browser for bonus material on my website: TomatoPasteLeadership.com/bonus.

INGREDIENT 2:
Strategic Objective

"'Would you tell me, please, which way I ought to go from here?'

'That depends a good deal on where you want to get to,' said the Cat.

'I don't much care where—' said Alice.

'Then it doesn't matter which way you go,' said the Cat."

—Lewis Carroll, *Alice in Wonderland*

Back to my Disney trip: As I walked through the Magic Kingdom, my mind was still on ideas to do something new. As sweat rolled down our backs in 100-degree temperatures and 80 percent humidity, holding our daughters' little hands, I couldn't stop thinking about what they'd called my attention to. I had a thousand thoughts going through my head.

What do I want my life to look like?

What experiences do I want to create with my family?

How do I become the father I want to be?

How do I grow a company with the values I can taste, smell, and feel?

What do I want my business to look like?

What contribution do I want to make to my clients, employees, and community?

My business mindset started to change in Tomorrowland. From the moment I became a partner, I wanted to grow the business into a great company. I was going to do that.

While strolling with my family, I knew I was missing something.

My journey started with finding the pieces of the business puzzle. More importantly, I wanted more in life. Like my father before me, I wanted to be a present father, husband, and son to my family.

Of course, as my dad said, I was full of enough "piss and vinegar" running the company. I believed I could do both. What did I know? It's a good thing I was taking stupid pills back in my Learning Domenic days.

At least I knew how to fix the present problem and improve things with my girls. Another thing I learned from my dad, my best mentor: when in doubt, ice cream!

"Hey, monsters, does anyone want ice cream?"

"Yeahhhhhhh, Daddy, Daddy, Daddy!"

Watching my daughters paint their faces with Mickey Bars put a heart-warming smile on my face.

I was excited. I knew my daughters had opened me up to new possibilities. I thought about the power of the mind—hear me roar.

I am a voracious reader. I have already read several influential books, like *How to Win Friends and Influence People* by Dale Carnegie, *The Magic of Believing* by Claude M. Bristol, *Awaken the Giant Within* by Tony Robbins, and one of my favorites, *Think and Grow Rich* by Napoleon Hill.

I had an epiphany. I needed my business to support my life—to work around my life rather than my life existing to support the business. A thriving business was a part of this life. I had to support my family. Yet I believed that I could do both. (Spoiler: it is possible. It was possible. I did what was possible. I now coach the possible. I am right.)

Looking back at Learning Domenic, I realize the possibility became more apparent once I found my Purpose in Life. My Purpose in Life and values of family, health, learning, and business building helped me know who I am, my purpose, and my direction. I knew where I was going in life!

Now, I needed a map to guide me toward one of my purposes in life: growing a great organization, not just for myself but also for my family, employees, and community. I was thinking big time while enjoying a Mickey Bar with my monsters.

That's what a Strategic Objective will do for your organization.

What my purpose in life did for me is what Strategic Objectives and values will do for your company and the people who touch it.

This strategy is a clear, written statement of what your organization will look and act like in the *future*—a treasure map of the business' future direction.

Can you imagine? Everyone in your company is on the same page. They know who they are, what services they provide, who they serve, where the company is going, and when it will get there. They also know how they will grow.

I know you want this business to grow right now, and another planning tool doesn't always seem like it'll get you there. I, too, wanted action. I wanted speed.

I needed all the things you need.

I'm here to tell you that a simple, well-written Strategic Objective gives your organization the sense of direction it needs. It is the starting point for all the decision-making, planning, and systems your organization needs, and it is where we will start building your company.

Key Concepts

- **Uniting Force:** A Strategic Objective is the battle cry that brings your business together and drives you toward growth—for everyone. Everything you do moves you toward this vision.

- **Keep It Simple:** Your Strategic Objective is a clear one-page statement of what your company would look and act like if your business were in the future.

- **Goals Can Be Achieved:** Purposes don't go away like goals do; they guide your life. Your Strategic Objective is like the goals that help you guide your business toward your Purposes in Life.

- **Stay Honest:** A Strategic Objective is not worth the paper printed on if it's not written honestly and made part of your living, breathing culture.

- **Lead by Objective:** No matter what you write down on your Strategic Objective, the secret for you as a leader is how you act and mentor your employees with this visionary document.

CHAPTER 5:
What Is a "Good Business"?

"Ever since I was a child, I have had this instinctive urge for expansion and growth. To me, the function and duty of a quality human being is the sincere and honest development of one's potential."

—Bruce Lee

How often have you heard, "You need to stop working *in* your business and start working *on* it"?

Or "What got you here won't get you there"?

These quotes sound great, but WTF do they even mean?

I have another way to frame them. Owners are too busy working in their unmanageable companies to find the time to build toward anything more significant. Even if they want to, there is little to no time to work on growing the business, let alone to spend with family.

With the second quote, you can't act exactly as you did when you first started and managed your company—back when it was manageable. Well, you could, but you would not be as successful.

Let's not get to the terrifying suspicion that we may not have the skill set to grow the company. That is precisely where I was in Tomorrowland—I knew how to run a company but didn't know how to grow one. The terrifying part for me was that "I is an engineer." How could I not know?

Growing up in my dad's business taught me how to run a business. I learned many aspects of accounting, bookkeeping, scheduling, management, ordering, purchasing, client management, machine maintenance, and more. It was an education second to none.

I joined my dad's partnership after college. We enjoyed breaking the $1 million sales barrier and landing in the $2 million sales arena. Our collaboration was where my dad first commented on how "full of piss and vinegar" my work personality was. We had an excellent opportunity to sell our organization to a national company without knowing or understanding what happened at a certain growth point in that business. The statement "what got you here won't get you there" didn't come into play. We grew to a level that two owners could manage.

At my Tomorrowland crossroads, those issues became apparent. I didn't realize that a command-and-control management style would not work for the next level we wanted to reach. I could not just do more of everything and manage more of everything and still build a more prominent, better organization, let alone be part of my family.

I knew why I wanted to do all of it. I had my Purpose in Life.

I even knew a bit about what to do. I ran and sold a successful $2 million company.

I didn't know what to *stop* doing or how to start growing.

Once you've named your Purpose in Life and seen where your life and business are out of alignment, that busy work isn't so satisfying anymore. You know there's something more out there for you, and you know what you are doing this for.

The catch is that you must slow down to find that "more," and you only have so much time in a day.

You're working *in* the business to keep it going, even though you want to work *on* the business to make it everything you dream it could be.

The good news is the exciting next step will help you start working *on* more and *in* less.

The not-so-exciting news is you'll have to keep working for a while longer.

A Speaker at a Landscape Conference Breaks the News

Back from our first beautiful Disney World trip and away from Tomorrowland, I was still immersed in the daily grind, working around the clock. I was armed with a newfound purpose. Working with the vigor of "piss and vinegar," I was on a mission to find answers wherever I could.

At the time, we had minimal resources to afford the pooh-bah consultants of the day. Instead, I turned to the next best thing: devouring more books and attending countless industry conferences. I loved those events. They were a perfect place to think outside the box and let my imagination run free. They also allowed my partner and me to escape the daily questions and struggles at work.

Once there, I would seek out as many successful business owners as possible. One thing that I admire about successful owners is their openness to helping others.

A recurring theme echoed through these halls: *systems!*

Systems were touted as the holy grail of business growth, the key to unlocking success. No matter the question, the answers were always the same: systems, systems, systems.

What the hell do I know? Let's go back to the company and start building systems.

I attended one such conference and was captivated by one of the speakers. He was a young entrepreneur who had achieved remarkable success in the landscaping industry. He described how he built his company to $15 million, sold it, and was on a new path to creating an entrepreneurial program on the college level—a very new idea in the 1990s.

His journey resonated deeply with me. I aspired to do precisely what he'd done, to accomplish the same transformative path to creating a successful business and becoming a teacher and mentor for others.

After his presentation, I mustered the courage to approach him and ask him if my partner and I could get some advice.

For the price of a cup of coffee, I asked him, "How did you do it?" (Can you imagine me asking this stupid question? What on earth would he tell us in thirty minutes? I hate to say it, but I was looking for that magic pill.)

Instead of answering, he patiently asked us who we were, what we did, and how we ran the business.

I poured out my ambitions: I wanted a business that thrived and wholeheartedly served its clients. I craved grand success, but I was unsure of the path ahead.

I felt like an excited little schoolboy, telling him everything, hoping he would see how hard we worked. Then I said proudly, "We are the ones in charge."

He paused, and as I waited for him to provide this magic pill, he asked, "In charge of what?"

His question pierced through me.

At that moment, he revealed a stark truth: our business was merely a facade. We were the business juggling every aspect of its operation without a sustainable framework. Our hard work sustained the illusion of success, but a glaring void lay beneath the surface.

He smiled and put his finger to his mouth, saying, "Shhhhhhh-hhh. I won't tell anyone."

It seemed that *shhhhhh* sound went on forever in my mind—and still does.

He continued, "I can see that you are two hardworking men who care for your clients. So, let's keep this our secret."

His words shook me to the core. They shattered my illusions of grandeur and laid bare the reality of our situation. We had a *facade* of a great company!

The surprising part was that he was absolutely right. My partner and I were the systems. We did everything—sales, production, accounting, bookkeeping, ordering, etc. We were the business. What was our specialty? We commanded and controlled the hell out of our employees. Remove us, and there would be nothing left to run the company.

He gave us some ideas on how to make that change. He had some books to read and a consultant or two he knew were good—ideas about workable systems, employee development, and, of course, becoming a leader.

We thanked him for his thoughts and help. We left and continued walking through the conference halls.

As we walked, I couldn't shake off what he had said.

I told my partner, Joseph, that the meeting had really bothered me. *Holy shit.* I did not want to be the owner who just talked about the big game of our business. I didn't want to puff my chest out talking to other business owners about our successful business and big-time gross sales.

I did not want to run a facade. The realization that we were merely masquerading as a successful business troubled me.

My partner told me it didn't bother him and not to let it bother me. He said, "Sales is what makes a business. We can fake the rest."

I was dumbfounded, still reeling from what the conference speaker had said, and now this!

I *did* let it bother me. For the rest of the conference, I thought about it, searched and searched, took as many notes as possible, and looked for the breadcrumbs of success.

The speaker's and my partner's words had stirred something within me—a resolve to transcend the facade and transform our company into a genuine force to be reckoned with.

Who Are You, and What Do You Do?

When the speaker asked us about our business, I told him everything I thought he needed to know.

I worked *in* it, thinking I was ready to work *on* it.

Looking back now, as Teaching Domenic, it's clear to me what this speaker was alluding to: we wanted him to tell us how to grow, but we couldn't even tell him who we were, much less what growing would look like for us. If we'd known who we were, what services we provided, where we were going, and why we wanted to grow, that conversation with He would have gone differently.

I found out that we needed a Strategic Objective. It was the beginning of our stellar growth.

A Strategic Objective is a clear, one-page written statement outlining what your organization will become, how it will look, and how it will operate in the future. I emphasize the word 'will' because this step isn't about wishful thinking or simply reflecting the status quo. It's about making a deliberate decision on who you are, what you do, where you're headed, when you'll arrive, and a clear vision of the future company. This distinction is crucial, and I'll expand on it in this section.

If you were building a house, would you pay some tradespeople to show up and start working? Would you tell the builder, the plumber, and the electrician that you want "a home" and then just let them go to work? That would be ridiculous. I doubt there is a house built in the world that didn't start with an image of what it would look like when finished and written plans to ensure everyone stayed on course.

If there were homes like this, I wouldn't want to live in one.

Building a successful business is much more complicated than building a house. Yet most business owners do it daily without clear plans.

When the conference speaker asked us to tell him about our business, I didn't see it as who we served or how we did it—I saw it as a million little things that had to be done daily.

In the same way that I don't coach people without first understanding why they want to grow—what their Purpose in Life is—he couldn't teach me how to develop a business that I couldn't even define.

If you want to build a successful business that doesn't collapse around you or trap you inside for the rest of your life, you need a plan. You need to know what your business will look like when it's "finished."

Strategizing for the Future

The vision of a Strategic Objective does not just materialize overnight or even in a year. The beauty of looking into the future is that we can see what needs to happen incrementally to reach the ultimate goal.

For example, say your company is presently at $1 million in sales. You have a Strategic Objective to be a $3 million company in five years. It isn't about becoming a $3 million company overnight but knowing that your goal is $3 million and moving forward one year at a time. You are planning many aspects of the company each year. In the fifth year, your plans and results

may give you a company that looks, feels, acts, and tastes like—
and is—a $3 million company.

In each area of a Strategic Objective, the owners and the employees can see what they need to do and when. When something smacks you on the side of the head or something that will help you with these objectives comes across your theoretical desk, you know how to decide which can help or hinder. That decision or choice is based on what you know and how you envision your future organization.

I am getting ahead of the how-to that's still to come, but it's essential to understand that we're not just jotting down a pie-in-the-sky wish.

A simple, one-page Strategic Objective answers the following questions:

- **Who** will the company be when we reach the Strategic Objective? Who are the clients? Who are the employees?

- **What** services does the company provide?

- **When** will we reach the sales goal for the Strategic Objective? When will we reach the net goal?

- **Where** are we located? Where are the clients located?

- **Why** does the company exist?

For the owner, a written Strategic Objective is taken out of their head and clearly shows what the company will "look, act, smell, taste, and feel like in the future"—and how it will perform. These objectives are what have been in your head forever. Now they are written and clear, and you, as the owner, have set the company's direction.

For the employee, it provides a sense of direction—a way to see themselves as part of the journey toward the organization's future. The employees do not need to read the owners' minds. They do not have to guess about what they are doing or why. Their mission is clear.

Without a Strategic Objective, it's challenging to articulate your business' identity and direction.

Let's look at some tactical areas in the Strategic Objective that can guide you *in* the business:

- You'll be able to build systems that will run the company in the future and give you the results the company must achieve instead of creating a system to work today.

- You'll know what resources to buy and when—including equipment, computers, buildings, and materials.

- You'll know which employees you need to hire and when.

- You'll know what each department consists of and needs to be within that future company.

- You'll have a clear idea of your finances and if you can you buy everything you need when you need it.

You will also be able to start working *on* your company. Here are some questions to ask yourself in preparation for the strategic work that you will be doing:

- Are you ready to manage more people? Do you need more leadership skills?

- Do you have the kind of clients to reach that target? How will you find and nurture more clients?

- Do you have employee development that will give your employees the skills they need to satisfy the clients?

- What systems and processes do you need to make the company more consistent and streamlined?

If your yearly goals are not accomplished, there's nothing wrong with reducing your target revenue, stretching the goal to five years instead of three, adjusting and rerouting the direction, and so on.

When I workshop this with people, it's not uncommon for the numbers to change once we consider what it'll take to achieve them. While $3 million might feel out of reach until we break it down into a year-by-year set of objectives, sometimes that breakdown shows us our numbers aren't realistic.

This will be a prolonged learning process, but when you know where you are going, you can take advantage of opportunities as they appear.

As valuable as it is to have a way to make decisions, the benefits of a Strategic Objective are even better in reverse: when you start changing systems, hiring people, and refining flows, everyone in the organization will already know why. And they should be just as excited about it as you are.

A Strategic Objective is the battle cry that brings your business together and drives you—and everyone else—toward growth.

How Do Goals Work with Purposes?

Before we move on to examples and set your Strategic Objective in motion, let's briefly discuss goals and purposes. I always get this question: what is the difference between goals and purposes?

Goals have a beginning and end; purposes do not.

When you want to buy a car, you set a goal and take steps to achieve it. Once you get the car, the goal is met. The Purpose may have been to travel, and that purpose will be forever. Buying a car is a goal.

When I set a goal to become a better leader for my company and employees, I needed to read books and audiobooks, attend seminars and conferences, ask for help, and hire an executive coach. Those choices helped me reach my goal of becoming a better leader, yet my Purpose in Life of learning is forever.

Goals direct our choices in the short term; keeping those choices in alignment with our Purpose in Life shapes the long term. And those purposes don't ever go away. They guide your whole life.

Remember that your Purpose in Life and goals are entirely personal to your life and what you want it to look, feel, taste, and be like. Your Strategic Objective is more like detailed goals for your company. Your Strategic Objective has a start and end time, and you and your team can visit these goals periodically. When you reach the end of the future company, it will be time to create a new strategy for a new future.

Sometimes, it becomes clear that growth goals aren't just about money—they're about designing a life that works for you. I am one of those cases. As the company's goals were updated with the Strategic Objective, growth became about creating an environment for everyone to thrive.

Our goals change with every new five-year Strategic Objective, but my purpose, which is the company values and culture of a great, successful organization, does not. A purpose is forever.

The idea is to use both of these tools to envision and create a life you'd love to live—the kind of life you're striving for—one goal at a time.

CHAPTER 6:
How to Build a Living Strategic Objective

"When your values are clear to you, making decisions becomes easier."

—Roy E. Disney

Look at a finished Strategic Objective statement from one of my past partnerships. I share this example not because the Strategic Objective is a particularly challenging step but because it's easy to get lost in the details if you don't know what you're going for. The most important things to pay attention to are what "writing for the future" means and how specific your answers are.

You can follow along using the who, what, where, when, and why questions or download a copy of a template at TomatoPasteLeadership.com/bonus.

Write yours as we go if you haven't answered each W question already, or follow along as we break down this Strategic Objective statement, piece by piece, before working on your own.

Ready?

Here's the first part:

> In 2019, BEST Professional Grounds Services is a premier, full-service grounds management team providing services to high-end residential estates and homes in the Greater Tri-State Area. Through our Southbury, Con-

necticut, headquarters location, with over thirty-five employees, we experience annual sales of $3 million with a net profit of 20 percent.

Our professional services include outstanding niches in garden and flower management, lawn services, pesticide management, and snow and ice management. While we serve high-end residential clients during the summer, in the winter, our snow and ice management services focus mainly on commercial clients.

How many W questions did you see baked into this part of the statement?

- **Who** is the company? It is a premier, full-service grounds management team.

- **Who** are our clients? They are high-end residential estates and homes, in summer, and commercial clients in winter.

- **What** do we provide clients? We provide snow and ice management, garden management, lawn services, pesticide management, and snow removal services.

- **When** will we reach our profit objective? In 2019, annual sales are $3 million with a net profit of 20 percent.

- **Where** are our clients located? The clients are located in Connecticut, New York, and Massachusetts.

- **Where** are we? We work from the headquarters in Southbury, Connecticut.

Getting the hang of it?

Note that each sentence in the Strategic Objective is written in the present tense, not the future. Even though we were in 2014, we were acting and living as if we were the future company. This is fundamental to the process because the Strategic Objective allows future goals to guide present actions and decisions. It's not just a distant dream. You want to read it as an active statement about who, what, when, where, and why you are. Use it to think and act like the company, employees, and owner you want to be instead of acting from where you are right now.

Here's the following section:

> We acquire and retain long-term relationships with our residential and commercial clients. Our target residential clients are between the ages of thirty and fifty, married unless at the younger end of the age group, well-educated millionaires who want luxury items and nothing but the best.
>
> We position ourselves in the market as a company with a wealth of knowledge and phenomenal expertise in landscape architecture and installation, lawn and pesticide management, irrigation, arborists' needs, and gardening. If we don't have the knowledge, we know someone who does.

This part focused on one kind of W question. Did you catch it?

- **Who Our Clients Are:** They are between the ages of thirty and fifty and married unless at the younger end of the age group. They are well-educated millionaires who want luxury items and nothing but the best. We also have commercial accounts for snow removal.

- **Who Our Employees Are:** People with common sense, knowledge, and phenomenal expertise.

With that 'Who' still in mind, this Strategic Objective ends with a vision of who the employees are:

> Our employees are well-groomed and dressed according to the company's dress code. They are well-trained through fifty-two weekly sessions of our BEST University education programs; they are safety-minded, hard-

working, ready to work, polite, and reliable. All our employees reflect self-generated pride in their work with us.

Our office complex looks like a home away from home: clean, organized, structured, and efficient. Our state-of-the-art trucks and equipment are well-maintained and managed for safety and efficiency. They are always sparkling clean and neatly stored.

We employ a systematic business development process to realize our Strategic Objective. All employees are involved in the business and the systems development process. We continually execute innovative approaches to guarantee our ability to respond to our customers immediately. In addition, our foremen employ superior monitoring of all aspects of our services to ensure we always serve our clients, period!

This one's more tricky because it explains the company's values, culture, and whys, which we'll unpack more soon. In the meantime, can you spot any indicators of the company's values?

- **Image:** Our employees are well-groomed and follow a dress code. Our office is clean, organized, structured, and efficient. Our trucks and equipment are always sparkling clean and neatly stored.

- **Education:** We have fifty-two weekly sessions of our BEST University education programs.

- **Employee Development:** Our employees are career-developed and position-trained to run the systems.

- **Systems Run the Company:** Employees are involved in the business and the systems development process. Our company is system-managed, not people-managed.

- **Top Value:** We always serve our clients, period!

Emphasis on Strategy

When I work with owners, I do not want to squash their dreams. As a coach, I have seen the impossible goals owners set and the havoc it causes when they try to go after them. I have seen whole companies implode from underserved clients and unsustainable practices. I have seen good employees leave because of the crazy demands put on them. I even had to stop coaching some companies because of the owners' unrealistic dreams and unrestrained egos.

I have also seen some lofty goals accomplished. I love it when an organization has that "shoot for the stars because if you miss, you might land on the moon" belief. There is a difference between the belief that you should shoot for the stars and going after something unrealistic that could destroy you.

The following table demonstrates how I have coached companies toward solid, workable goals. It is a list of key indicators that correspond to the vision of your Strategic Objective, turning it into the results and benchmarks needed to make that future your reality.

To learn more about your Strategic Objective, click here or put the link in your browser for bonus material on my website: TomatoPasteLeadership.com/bonus.

The table is divided into two columns. On the left are the key indicators of the present company—gross sales, net profit percentage, employees needed, resources needed, systems to be created/updated, financial needs, and project agendas. On the right is what you will be and look like in your when—your future company.

For each key indicator, the needs of that year are broken down so that everyone will know what the company needs to be doing each year:

- Currently, the organization is a $1 million company in 2014. The "out of the box" challenging growth goal of $3 million in five years is shown on the right.

- Gross sales need to increase by approximately $250,000 annually to $1.25 million in 2015, $1.5 million in 2016, and $3 million in 2017.

- The net profit percentage indicator increases by an average of 3 percent. As the company becomes more effective and consistent, it jumps to 5 percent in 2015.

- Employees will be added for the company to satisfy the $250,000 increase in sales.

- Equipment, trucks, and office indicators show what resources must be added annually.

- Systems are evaluated yearly, and an agenda is created for what systems need to be built to handle $3 million.

This table becomes your plan to implement the Strategic Objective. This table will also help you with a reality check. Before you finalize this plan, can you add that many employees? That much equipment? Or does your plan need to be adjusted?

Once it's finalized, the whole company can see each year's agenda at a glance, without any doubt about their direction, what to do, and when to do it.

Of course, let's not kid ourselves. Just writing down a list of goals and values isn't where the magic is. This kind of statement *can* be total BS if it's not part of your daily business life. It has to be put into action.

Your Strategic Objective in Action

While on vacation with my family, I visited a Ben & Jerry's in Lake George, New York. (Perhaps I should have named this book *Ice Cream Leadership!*) As we stood in line, the girls bounced around and talked about what flavors they might get, while I noticed a mural on the wall.

To my surprise, that beautiful painting was a statement of the company's values, not unlike a Strategic Objective. It said how they started, who they were, and what they are today. What a beautiful company story. They also had what they believed in today and how they would continue. *We believe in this, and we will always do that.* Well, I had to ask the cashier about it.

Okay, okay. I had to be an ass about it.

I wanted to prove something to myself. I didn't think for a second that those people knew who they were and what they believed, even with it on the wall.

So, without pointing to the painting, I asked, "What is your Strategic Objective in this place? What do you all believe?"

Chirp, chirp, chirp.

Yes, it's a silly point to make in an ice cream shop. However, I find the same thing to be true in most organizations. The owner *loves* to tell you what they believe in. If it's not hanging on the wall somewhere, it's on their website or how they talk about their business.

"We believe in the employee." Yet one can observe how the employees are treated, which isn't like the gold they are.

"We believe in the client." Yet do we give them that "client is always right" 100 percent?

"We care about the environment." Yet if we can find a bargain with lesser-quality materials, do we buy them?

"The systems run our company." Yet we are there running everything, one command after another.

It seems that the Strategic Objective is not worth the ink it's printed with—or the paint on the wall, as it were—if it's not written honestly and made part of your daily routine.

How you use this document is key to its success. The Strategic Objective should not be merely a document but a living, breathing part of the organization's culture and practices.

A strategy is a story reinforced through every department, operational detail, and customer experience. When you ask anyone in the organization, any team member, who we are, who our clients are, where we are, what we do, and when we will arrive at our destination, they should have a complete, transparent understanding.

This Strategic Objective, these values, are what becomes your map and your culture.

You are now armed with your Purpose in Life, your life map. You are armed with a Strategic Objective, the company's map. You are armed with values to mentor and develop the culture. These are the beginning tools of a Tomato Paste Leader: the leader who has created a clear vision for the organization and rallies employees toward common goals.

In particular, the Strategic Objective and Company Values serve as a unifying force that motivates employees and guides their actions toward growth and success. Writing out the Strategic Objective isn't meant to show off something meaningless. It takes that vision out of your head and makes it available to your employees so they don't have to read your mind anymore. So you don't wind up building the facade of a great company that only you can run.

CHAPTER 7:
Values Become Culture

"Act the way you'd like to be, and soon you'll be the way you'd like to act."

—Leonard Cohen

After the conference, where we sat with this extraordinary speaker, my partner and I returned home. As soon as we turned the key to the office door, we were thrust back into the same muck, facing the same problems.

I had a new outlook. I was seeing the hours and resources we were spending through a different lens.

We weren't busy because "that's what good owners do." We were busy because the work was too chaotic and only getting more confusing.

Paperwork was not coming to me correctly and on time, and work orders were unclear or incomplete. I needed more information and had to chase people down every single night. Employees required more information and waited for us to spell it out every second. Even though we needed more, better-trained employees, we didn't know how to take on more work with more people. We had next to no time to build or think.

I have to smile thinking about how Dad would say we did "everything from cleaning the toilets to signing the checks." He would also call us glorified workers—we were owners, but making all the decisions and doing whatever it took to make the company run made us the busiest "employees" on staff.

I was stressed, wanted to spend more time with family, and tired of presenting myself as a successful business owner.

Meanwhile, my partner was still doing just fine as a workaholic (hell, since I worked 24/7, I was one, too). We started arguing more and more, and our Italian tempers could fly at any moment.

We were making good money, but it was costing us our sanity.

While learning as much as I could from books, I realized I had a hidden value.

My value of growing a business for myself and my partner became more than just running a business. It was to establish a company known for its thriving culture.

I am sure it came from my dad's mentorship and example as an owner, father, husband, veteran, and teacher. I remember his one value as an owner was to ensure that local people had jobs and training. He would say these people had "good hands" when speaking about their talents. He would say that they were hidden gems.

I didn't know it then, but I had the same values deeply embedded in my soul. I wanted to foster an environment where everyone thrived financially and professionally, all while being committed to delivering exceptional service to our clients.

Values Anchor the Strategy

A Strategic Objective is not something you put in a manual to reference once or paint on a wall to showcase to everyone. It is something that everyone has to strive for. It is always in your mind and the minds of your employees. It is what a leader leads toward.

For a while, I thought having good intentions as an owner was enough. I made sure to behave and work in a certain way—always ensuring I completed the job, talking to clients in a specific manner, filling my work orders, setting my truck up, etc.

You get the picture. I acted in a way that made my values obvious, thinking this would teach the employees how to act and work.

I believed they could read my thoughts.

In 1996, I hired a strategy coach. She began in a unique way that I have carried with me when coaching clients: with why. What was to be a one-week project turned into a month-long project. Somewhere deep down, I knew that I needed to get this right.

Later, I found that my whys (my Purpose in Life) became the company's culture and values.

I wrote those values down and determined they would permeate the company and my employee interactions. Not surprisingly, while each Strategic Objective changed after each period's completion, the values we named at the beginning of this work did not change. Those values—which were part of me and what I believed in—lasted throughout my partnerships and remain even today in my coaching work:

1. **Service the Client, Period:** This service includes vendors, employees, and subcontractors, not just those we typically think of as clients.

2. **Systems Run the Company:** We use systems, flows, and consistent templates to serve the client.

3. **Trained, Position-Oriented People Run the Systems:** We strive to improve ourselves through communication, management, system training, and anything that can help us improve.

4. **Education:** We believe in career development, from hiring and orientation to the continuing working years. Our mission with this value is to create an environment where we all can thrive.

5. **Image:** Everything, everyone, in every place, looks and acts the best way possible.

When you embody your company's stated values and constantly mentor employees toward those values, you are nurturing a culture of growth and excellence. When you are passive about those values, keeping them to yourself and hoping your people will read your mind, you run into what my partner and I did when we talked to that speaker at the landscape conference. We couldn't tell anyone where we were going or why. I didn't even know my partner's thoughts on where he envisioned us going until I saw him shrug off the idea that we were a facade.

We weren't on the same page about what "making the company run" meant. We understood that we were working hard to make a good living, but we hadn't communicated about anything else. Looking from the outside at how we ran the company, you could see what we stood for: hard work, getting it done, and dependability. My partner and I were the frontmen. We made it a strong company. Behind closed doors, however, we spun in circles around each other and the business as Tasmanian Devils. We were command-and-control owners controlling everything and everyone. Employees waited for us to give them what to do and when. Our chaos *was* the culture.

Unfortunately, you don't have to name or write down your values to have values in your company. *Not* writing down a vision or values doesn't keep you from having a company culture. It will develop independently, matching the way the owner acts.

Similarly, writing down your Strategic Objective and not utilizing it will not introduce a direction for your organization. Using this map will point you in a more intentional direction so you can know and name who you are, who your clients are, and what services you provide. You will know where your clients live, work, and play. You can understand and name why you exist as a company.

Naming (and Living by) Your Values

The Ws of a Strategic Objective tell us who our clients are, what services we offer, where we're going, and when we will get there as an organization. In the example in the previous chapter, we broke down those Ws. We also saw what might be the most *crucial* part of a Strategic Objective. It appeared in the paragraphs where image, education, systems, and service emerged. These are the values that drive the actions of your company. Your Company Values make the Strategic Objective so strategic. It's why you exist and how you will act out your Strategic Objective.

Technically, you could—maybe even should—write your Company Values before writing your Strategic Objective. After all, as we'll soon see, your values come from your Purpose in Life. Your Company Values are to your company what your Purpose in Life is to you.

You can just as quickly start with your company's who, what, where, and when and work backward to find the why of your company. Let's be honest: after all that introspection around Purpose in Life, it's nice to take a moment to talk about what is essential to the business you are building.

The order of operations to create your Strategic Objective and Company Values isn't as important as understanding that your values are why you exist as you follow the path marked out on the map of your Strategic Objective. It's how you act and behave as you get to that destination. It's how you become more than just a facade.

When the conference speaker discussed how we weren't a business, he communicated a value. My partner indicated his values when the conversation didn't bother him. For him, a company was anything that made a profit, even if it was an illusion behind closed doors. For me, a great company created an environment where everyone could thrive professionally and financially, where systems ran the day-to-day, and where people knew what to do and how.

For twenty-seven years, my partner and I came together to create our Strategic Objective. Yet, our values were incompatible from the start. My leadership and the employees under me imitated the values I lived and breathed. With my partner, his employees followed and imitated the values he lived and breathed.

The actual values, like it or not, are how a leader acts, not what they say or write.

Suppose an owner is only interested in making money. In that case, the bottom line becomes their most important concern, and an "every person for themselves" culture forms.

Suppose an owner screams commands to manage the company. In that case, they'll have a culture of tension and people waiting for their next orders to follow.

If an owner is passive, their culture will be unpredictable, subject to whatever whims they allow.

You may want to change your behaviors to create a more intentional, thriving culture. That's great—it's why you're here. Unfortunately, none of us are mind readers, especially your employees. So, you're here to do the hard work of writing it down, saying it aloud, acting on those behaviors, and mentoring your employees with these values.

The hard work is not just figuring out what kind of company you want; it's making your values clear enough—on paper and in practice—for others to see that you hold yourself to what you believe and join you in it.

Take the "image" value, for example. When I said "image" was one of my values, I was talking about *everything*. Everything was to be pristine and organized, from the toilets to the trucks to the office. All the production employees needed to be in the same (clean) uniform. Each foreman organized their trucks and equipment for a professional appearance.

This value also included how employees worked in the office or how clean their desks were at the end of a workday.

I learned a technique and taught this value from a coach in the coaching organization around *Getting Things Done* by David Allen: I kept only active paperwork on my desk, and all other projects stayed filed until I worked on them.

This was how I acted, as well as how I trained and mentored my employees.

Mina, the first person I trained to take over my position as liaison manager in the office, took the values to another level. One morning, something seemed off with my protégé. I strolled by her desk, amazed that every space on the desk and the floor was *filled* with paperwork. This was unusual for her. Usually, she worked on only what was needed and kept all else filed or stored.

"Mina, what on earth happened? You seem overwhelmed with work. How can I help?"

She said, "I'm all set. Your partner is coming into the office today."

"Then why the hell does your area look like a cyclone hit it? How do you know that my partner is coming in? And what does it have to do with your desk?"

She added, "Look down the hall at your partner's executive administrator."

Sure enough, his executive administrator had everything on the desk and floor, strewn laughably down the hall.

Mina knew my partner's unspoken value: "Being busy or looking busy means you're being productive."

Like it or not—whether you name your values or not—your values become your culture.

The differences between my values and my partner's values were apparent. Eventually, my values helped and guided me to sell my partnership. This contrast is something to be aware of as you get more intentional within your company. Ignoring the real problems lurking under the surface only causes them to get more challenging and complex over time.

CHAPTER 8:
Leaders Go First

"A leader is one who knows the way, goes the way, and shows the way."

—John C. Maxwell

After fifteen years of working and running my companies, my passion evolved. While I still loved the physical work, I discovered a more profound love for teaching and mentoring my employees.

Unfortunately, changes were also happening around me. My partner and I began to diverge in our values and vision for the company.

My partner and I had reached the top of our game. In less than ten years, our team had placed us in the top 3 percent of North America's landscaping and snow removal businesses.

We made magic happen for some of the most beautiful properties you've ever seen. We also discussed an exciting new five-year strategic plan to grow from $15 million to $23 million.

The team was also excited about this growth. They knew they would be involved in creating, documenting, teaching, and implementing all the resources we would need to achieve this goal. I was looking forward to using my growing leadership and system development superpowers to make it happen.

However, my partner and I envisioned our $23 million organization differently. He prioritized profits for corporate owners, while I valued a community-minded approach that benefited everyone.

That business had provided me with a beautiful life, enabling me to be present for my daughters. Simple things like being home in the morning and on weekends, helping them with homework, taking them to dance recitals, and attending family functions.

It connected me to the Julios and Minas. It allowed me the opportunity to become the best leader.

The financial benefits gave me a house, an income, and bonuses that some would have said I'd be crazy to give up.

Partners need to share a unified vision, strategy, and culture. Over the last fifteen years of coaching, I've seen conflicting values in partnerships rarely work, and it didn't work for two of my partnerships.

I faced significant, life-changing choices.

How did I decide to continue or make a change? With the guidance of my mentors and the unwavering support of my wife, my rock, I was in good hands during this challenging period.

I also had an essential tool in my toolbox: my Purpose in Life. This Purpose in Life was my compass. They guided my decisions and ensured I stayed true to my values.

As hard as it was to leave the salary, benefits, security, and, most importantly, *the team* behind, it was clear that my Purpose in Life was not being satisfied. They were sending me in another direction.

I always ask clients why they want to grow before helping them achieve their goals. Business strategies must align with personal values, and misalignment between the two can lead to significant problems.

It is like the old story of painting a beautiful house only to discover that you painted the wrong house. One can build a fantastic business only to find out that it was not built to fulfill one's values.

I wanted to do something with what Learning Domenic had discovered and been taught by the many outstanding coaches I was blessed with. I wanted to become a Teaching Domenic who could bring that transformation to others.

So, I made the hard (yet correct) decision to sell all my shares of the three companies to my partner. I then went on a new, exciting two-year sabbatical to travel, get a master's degree in entrepreneurship, learn the online world, and set out in the new direction of building a coaching organization.

I put the same energy I'd put into the three organizations into the skills I needed to become the kind of coach I needed to find so many years ago: one who had experience growing profitable businesses, who had a proven map, who could guide me step by step, and who knew how all the pieces of the business puzzle came together.

That was almost fifteen years ago, and since then, I have coached many great companies and hundreds of entrepreneurs facing the same kind of dilemma I had. People who were growing their businesses and felt like something was still missing. Something they needed to transition toward.

To serve those people and stay in alignment with my purposes, I had to put my money where my mouth was; the coaching could only be part of my great successes in life.

Success looked like choosing to be the best husband and father to my wife and daughters and the best friend to my close friends that I could be. It was being a caregiver and companion to my mom and dad, helping them to the next life. It was learning how to make Italian delights, grow gardens, and make wine. It was jarring the best tomato paste with my family, with my favorite mom-in-law (my only, but still my favorite) at the helm.

When I coach, I look for owners who want success like that. Entrepreneurs who are seeking new knowledge, skills, and perspectives. People who are proactive in learning more and learning faster. Prosperity comes to people when they can absorb new ideas and filter out the ones that do not work for them anymore.

My success also included teaching owners who want to build something bigger than themselves. Owners who are willing to be open to new ways, able to make mistakes, and take ownership of those mistakes as just steps in the journey—owners who are growth-minded and have that great trait of teachability.

Of course, I help them make more profits. After interviewing many and taking only a few one-on-one clients, I can tell you that some owners want their business to grow into something special so that everyone can thrive—not just grow for growth's sake.

That's the type of person I mentor and coach.

OMG, Some Owners Never Learn

In the early coaching days, a close friend asked me to do him a favor.

He had a friend running a small landscape/snow company, and the owners needed some help. Of course, I said yes—I told them the consultation fee was a cappuccino, and we met at Starbucks.

There were two partners in this company. The older partner had been landscaping for about five years. He decided he needed help and added his brother-in-law as a partner. (Don't you love this family partner idea?) One worked in production, managing the crews in the field. He also did the sales and estimations. The other partner worked in the office, doing all the accounting and finance.

In the first year as partners, their sales hit about $350,000.

After I asked them why they wanted to grow—my go-to first question—they discussed many familiar issues: "Domenic, we are working 24/7. We are always in the office and the field." They wanted to know how to keep employees, manage their work, and make a profit.

They thought making more money would fix things.

After about half an hour, I asked one brother, "Kerry, what do you do?"

I got a puzzled look from Kerry, and then he blurted out, "I am the outside guy."

"But what do you do? What is your position?"

"I do the production and sales. I do everything outside."

I asked the other brother, "Edward, what do you do?"

The same puzzled look. "I'm the inside guy. I do all the office stuff."

"Well, what exactly?"

"Accounting and finance. I do everything inside."

There it was—the same facade the speaker from the conference saw in us. They didn't know what they were doing except trying to impress each other, show the other partner how much they did, and stay busy.

I helped them with a simple plan—not bad for two hours and a cappuccino—but they kept countering me with "I need this," "I need that," and "We do it this way!" All while going back to, "I know there must be a better way."

So, I left them with a smile, a bit of good luck, and the grim knowledge that businesses like theirs don't last long.

(A note about honesty when coaching: I am not there to powder your ass. I am there to assess, diagnose, offer solutions, and help you implement them. I am not your friend, though I am friendly and cordial. I am there, to be honest with you about where you are and help with solutions to where you want to go. I don't want to waste your money and my time.)

One year later, my friend, more handsome than the previous year, asked the same favor. (I am a glutton for punishment. You know, the type of guy who rubber-necks at a car accident. I wanted to find out what these owners were up to, plus enjoy a good coffee and a story.)

I sat in front of the same two owners. One shouted, "We grew 100 percent!" But in the same breath, sadly, and with a mumble, he added, "My wife is about to divorce me. I am always working, even when I am home."

They had the same questions about growth and the exact search for magic pills.

They got the same answers from me: positions, systems, and personal growth.

They responded the same way: "We see so many growing. What are we missing? What about the magic pill?"

This time, I went so far as to say that they needed to do things quickly in a new way. I told them outright, "You are heading for real problems." I could see the writing on the wall, and I told them I thought they might not make it past the following season.

Again, they thanked me, and off they went.

A year later, I got a phone call while I was outside weeding and staking my tomato plants. It was Kerry again.

"How are you doing? You won't believe it; we are at $750,000! Sadly, with one less partner."

Oh, really?

"Dom, you were right."

I hate that statement.

Kerry continued, "I am not sure, but I think I am making less profit than when I was at $350,000."

Kerry was generating more money but also working more hours and making less than he did when he first felt burned out. So I asked him again, "What on earth are you growing for?"

One suggestion (I knew he would not listen or implement my growth strategies) was to dial back to $350,000. He could make more profits and have more time with his wife and family.

As I waited out Kerry's silence, I listened to the sounds of my backyard.

Chirp, chirp, chirp of the birds.

Buzz, buzz, buzz of the bees.

A sweet breeze blew by.

He finally said, "And leave all that money on the table?"

After hanging up, I shook my head and thought, *OMG! Some owners will never learn.*

A few years after Kerry's last call, I asked my friend how Kerry was doing. My friend said, "He went out of business a few years ago. He is divorced, and I have not seen him yet."

Be Proud of Your Accomplishments

In another, happier encounter, I hired a new landscaper for my home in Connecticut. After watching all the action outside, I went to the front door, poked my head out, and asked the owner, Zeus, if he would like a cold drink for him and his men.

We talked about what he was doing with my property and his business. I let him know that I, too, owned a landscaping company and was fortunate to be part of such a brilliant collaboration in my company.

Then, as usual, I asked him some probing questions: "What made you get into this kind of work? What do you love about it? What do you hate about it?"

And then the disrupter: "Why do you want to grow?"

He stopped and pondered, then explained that, over the last three years, he had three trucks, two foremen with crews, and three sets of trucks, equipment, and tools.

I said, "You must be making close to $1 million in sales."

"How'd you know?"

I just did some arithmetic, and I've been there. The owner worked hard, had a good business, and worked for the right reasons: to create a great company and for his beautiful family.

Zeus continued, "But you know, Dom, I was making less than I did when I had just one truck and crew! I am sad that I am not spending time with my wife and three children. I am doing everything from sunup to sundown. My wife is trying to help me with the paperwork but is overwhelmed by family and work. It hurts not to be there. My kids are growing up without me."

You could see how deflated he was as he confided, "Dom, I had to go back to one truck and crew. You must look at me and think what an idiot, dumb businessman I am. I have a smaller company now than before!"

Zeus is precisely the kind of person I love to mentor. He is an entrepreneur who works hard and cares about his clients and employees.

I explained I knew how he felt. We were both looking for ways to become better.

I told him my story and the purpose I wanted to achieve. I explained how, over the years, I had attended many marketing, sales, and production seminars. Still, I became more confused and depressed.

I told him, "Zeus, you are one of the smartest owners I have been around lately. You knew something was not working for you even though you could puff your chest out with friends and associates about being a $1 million company. I have seen too many owners who don't dare to make good business choices to live the life they want to live. Be proud of your accomplishments and how successful you can be in your wife's and children's eyes. You are working less, making more profits, and finding more time for your wife and children."

I told him that I thought he'd made a good decision. You either find a new way to grow or grow to the level that makes the most sense for how you want to live. You are not afraid of either decision. He was brave enough to make the best decision for his life and family.

Zeus had his purposes and strategies; they may not have been written, but he needed to be more aware of them. I asked Zeus if he would like tools to create his Purpose in Life and set some business strategies. He welcomed them, and he went back to his work with a smile on his face.

After selling my companies, I was on the speaking circuit many moons later. Lo and behold, I saw the speaker from the conference who told me, "Shhhhhh, we won't tell anyone," sitting in the back row of one of my presentations.

Before I started, I walked over and reintroduced myself. I am sure He didn't recognize me. I had to tell him how much he helped me become a better leader and how I listened to his advice. I found the books and then a coach to help me. I was willing to put in the hard work and was grateful that he had pointed me in the right direction.

He did not realize how he did this or who I was. He had probably spoken to many owners who wanted the secrets of success in a thirty-minute session over coffee (just like I'd come to enjoy).

I don't know how that speaker felt during that brief encounter, but I can tell you how good it is to hear things like that from people I've coached or spoken with. It's far better than hearing, "Dom, you were right," from owners like Kerry. Fortunately, Kerry's fate isn't a necessary one. There is so much more to a business than its facade.

INGREDIENT 3:
Organizational Charts

"Another way to think of the WHY is as a piece of a jigsaw puzzle...and when others can see your piece, they can see whether it fits with theirs. If it does, that's when the image starts to take shape. In the real world, that looks like a team coming together to advance a common vision."

—Simon Sinek, *Find Your Why*

People are the lifeblood of your business, the driving force behind every operation, every decision, and every success.

It's worth saying that *people* run businesses.

Yet, in most organizations, the owner juggles many responsibilities. My dad would say that the owner wears many hats. In these companies (I am speaking from my own experience wearing many hats), the employees often learn how to act from the owners. They learn how to act and manage the same way as the owner, doing the same thing, wearing multiple hats, and waiting to be told what to do by the owners.

Furthermore, since everyone in the organization has multiple responsibilities, it's challenging for an owner to manage anyone toward results, mentor them, or find replacements when the time comes. Holding employees responsible for what they do or don't do becomes difficult. How could they do it when they don't know who is doing what or when they're doing it? Was it the mistake of this employee wearing this hat at this time or someone else?

The funny thing is, as the company grows and you want others to step up, you wonder why the employees cannot manage or do things unless you tell them. When the client list increases, the work increases, more employees are hired, and more resources are utilized. There is not enough time to manage everyone and everything. You start to lose control of the operation. You wonder why you are making more sales but less profits.

In contrast, within a thriving organization, individuals are assigned specific positions with specific roles tied to explicit results. In this environment, each employee understands their role not merely as a cog in a wheel but as an integral part of a collaborative system. They are part of a flow. The members and departments move within this company flow, depend on each other, and are united by shared objectives.

The leader plays a vital role in creating, nurturing, and leading employees in this environment—precisely what a Tomato Paste Leader is about.

The next step in your leadership journey is the construction of Organizational Charts, which are the visual representation of your organization. Organizational Charts are the roadmaps that guide every hiring decision and management action to get you to the Strategic Objective you just created.

Understanding structures is not enough; unlocking your team's full potential is crucial. The importance of role clarity, teamwork, and collaboration in achieving your vision of success cannot be understated.

This is where structure meets strategy.

Key Concepts

- **A Blueprint for Future Success:** Organizational Charts aren't merely diagrams. They are visual representations of how the organization should function and tools for guiding every facet of the business toward its Strategic Objective.

- **The Power of People:** People are the heartbeat of every business. They are the core of every organization. In a thriving organization, people run the systems that run the organization.

- **Role Empowerment:** Employees who clearly understand their place in the operation are not just assigned tasks but given owner-like decision-making powers.

- **A Culture of Collaboration:** Collaboration isn't just a buzz-word; it's the cornerstone of the organization's values and culture. Employees thrive in a collaborative environment.

- **Making Magic:** Organizational Charts serve as your North Star, revealing future pathways for career development. This is where the magic happens—where employees see their future.

CHAPTER 9:
Build from the Bottom Up

"Effectively, change is almost impossible without industry-wide collaboration, cooperation, and consensus."

—Simon Mainwaring

Determined to build a better business but unable to afford big-time consultants, I asked my dad for help. His advice was to start reading. He said a book was like a coach in a box and that good ones were the first place to find answers.

I read books on leadership, management, system development, and people development like a madman for the rest of that Tomorrowland year. I wanted to have a basic understanding of what other leaders were doing to become successful.

Hell, I wanted to know what they thought success was in the first place.

Meanwhile, out of nowhere, my partner—the man who had said, "Don't worry about creating a real business"—contacted the owner of one of Connecticut's most prominent landscape and snow removal companies to get his opinions about how to grow.

This prominent owner was glad to help us small potatoes figure out how to copy the big boys. He was kind enough to meet us at a diner in Shelton, Connecticut.

We waited for him in our little half-ton Datsun pickup truck (this was before I had named our value of maintaining an image, so even our trucks screamed mom-and-pop). This man drove up in a Cadillac and stepped out in a business suit.

We introduced ourselves in our typical garbagemen-green overalls and then followed him inside. *Holy shit.* I marveled at how this man must have become such a big success.

After we ordered coffee, he asked us about ourselves and our company.

He kept asking us questions and then rattling off ideas in response to our answers.

He talked about financials, employee hiring, systems development (how often I heard this "systems" mantra), and the importance of having multiple locations.

Then he asked for some water and pulled out a custom, designer packet of vitamins.

My head was spinning. Again.

There I was, waiting for the mother lode, the most magic of all magic pills, to grow a great company while he took his designer vitamins.

We had so far to go.

At some point, he paused and looked me in the eye. He pulled out a tattered paperback book, handed it to me, and told me to read it.

The book?

The E-Myth by Michael Gerber.

This kind owner offered a lot of advice, and we thanked him for his time, especially for the book—just like my dad's advice to read, read, and read some more.

I left with the book tucked under my arm, unsure what to make of a landscaper dressed in a suit and driving a Cadillac.

Unfortunately, that tattered book bored me to tears. As much as I tried, I couldn't understand what it was trying to say. I stored this on my bookshelf under the "someday maybe" area above my home office desk.

While I went back to "leading" my team to work our collective asses off and looking for more answers and solutions, my partner came back with another big idea. He caught me one afternoon and said, "Hey Dom, I was reading an ad in this landscape magazine. It has this man who says that he helps people with systems and organization. You know that the owner we met in Shelton, CT, believes systems are one of the ways to grow..."

This was the beginning of our foray into the world of consultants. A string of them soon followed.

We were naive and new to solving our growth issues, so hiring consultants to help us build some systems was a great place to start.

Sitting down to their brainstorming and creation phases was always interesting and exciting. Then, the real work came in as we attempted to implement the consultants' solutions, usually without the consultants. I had to double my workload with new routines and processes to follow while still keeping everything in check. Of course, we did some "training." But after a brief class on the system with the employees, we plunged headfirst, hopeful that this would be the time we'd finally improve the business.

When Systems Go First

Once, we worked with two consultants simultaneously—Joe and Fred—to implement two much-needed, separate systems. Joe's part was a work order system, and Fred's was an invoice system.

Joe started us off in the production area with a brilliant schedule board system and a simple work order template to support the production side. Because we were still doing the schedules, we enjoyed the fancy new boards and how much they helped us organize our work for the week. It was a great system that helped us see the bigger picture of our work.

Fred was Joe's cohort and came to us at Joe's recommendation. Fred did some great work in our sales and financial systems area, helping us create consistent sales quotes and proposals for what was, at that time, my partner's work.

We needed help brainstorming systems for better, quicker invoices and more substantial, robust, and consistent work orders. Joe and Fred each got to work, and we did our best to keep up.

I ran some classes for the employees and my partner (you can imagine the new "documenting, implementing, and teaching" hat I proudly wore).

About a month later, Joseph came to my office and frantically reported, "Domenic, the work orders don't work with my invoicing system. They're causing some enormous bottlenecks. I don't understand. WTF? Do something!"

Sure enough, the work orders I'd spent the last month implementing and teaching helped the production department but did more harm than good for the accounting department.

This time, I fully agreed with my partner, and as soon as the consultants returned—which was not soon enough—we directed our question to them: WTF?

Their answer?

"Dom, you didn't ask us to have the two systems to work together! We would have done that if you had said something!"

I am not a rocket scientist, but shouldn't the work orders work with invoicing? Shouldn't the last step in a work order system work with the first step in the invoice system?

I am sure you can see the humor in this moment, as I can now.

The owners must take responsibility for the results. Yet back then, I was pissed. *Really, guys?*

To their absolute credit, we had been struggling to break the $1 million mark in sales before we hired them. With a few new systems and fresh ideas, we were in the $2 million realm. What a few sound systems can do for you!

Another problem with the systems was that they helped my partner and me, not the employees. They only helped us because we were the company—we were using them to become more efficient. We were naive about how systems, employees, and flows should work in an organization and how we should use them.

We had a good team around us that yearned for more growth, but wanting to grow wasn't the same as being ready for growth. As soon as we acquired more clients and sales, we became overloaded, overworked, and unfocused—yet again!

Before we knew it, the magical systems were causing unexpected issues. Some employees tried to use the new systems, some only partially, and some returned to the old ways entirely.

Even worse, my partner would participate sometimes but not all the time. Couple that with his "get the f-ing work done" value that so many owners have, and it almost encouraged employees to cut corners around the systems.

Let's face it: employees will always gravitate toward the person who pays the checks.

I had thought our problems would go away as we hit new milestones. But the $2 million sales mark was just the first splashes of another rush of "whitewater rapids," stated a la Les McKeown's superb book *Predictable Success.*

We had entered into another arena. The paddles we once used to break the $1 million barrier didn't work in the new sales arena.

Why People Come First

Making more sales was not the same as making more profits. Our business became more chaotic, and my life became totally about my business.

This was not what I imagined "a better way" would be like.

Whenever we hired a new consultant to help us clean up the mess, I asked them the same question: "How do we bring it all together?"

Something had to be missing from all these systems we'd created. It couldn't *all* be my partner and me. God forbid.

Looking back on Learning Domenic, I wanted to know how people and systems work together, but I couldn't find the answer to the question as I do today as Teaching Domenic, "How do *people* and *systems* work together?"

Working late one night in my home office, about seven months after that prominent owner had coffee and vitamins with us, I pushed back in my chair and rubbed my head in tired anguish, looking up at the ceiling (or was it at heaven?), when something caught my eye.

The paperback book He had given me was still on my "some-day maybe" shelf above my desk.

I spied the book. The book spied on me.

I took a moment to pluck it off the shelf.

There must be something about this book.

This time, I read it.

Or should I say devoured it.

The E-Myth is about foundations, people, and strategies. It is about *owners.* I added these foundational strategies to my system-building skill set.

Systems are a bottom-up tool, and we were working top-down.

Let me explain. Owners are on top and commanding down. At the beginning of growth, owners use systems to be as effective as possible. The owners, in turn, command the employees to do every specific task.

Yet, bottom-up means that the company runs on systems, and the employees run the systems. In this way, you are in a bottom-up system process. You know you want to start growing your organization, and systems help the company do things more consistently.

All is well and good, but you, the owner, are not running these systems alone. You need your employees to run these systems if you want to be more effective and efficient and avoid doing every bit of work.

If we want people to run our systems, we need to start from the bottom up, where systems run the company and employees run the systems. This is the start of transforming an owner-run company into a system-run company.

To start this bottom-up process, you must determine who is responsible for what part of the system and ensure that they know how to perform their tasks consistently and effectively.

We will always pick up and wear many hats without Organizational Charts to give everyone specific positions and results. Organizational Charts and Positions are the tools to start this transformation.

With this knowledge, I could build a system, place it into a more extensive system flow, and watch the people I hired to do specific roles within that flow bring it all together.

Of course, this was not as simple as it sounds, but it was a start. We were starting to make art.

Now that you know where *you* are going (Purpose in Life) and where your business is going (Strategic Objective), it's time to visualize the team that will take you there from the bottom of the Organizational Charts up.

CHAPTER 10:
Charting the Internal Network

"Some changes look negative on the surface but you will soon realize that space is being created in your life for something new to emerge."

—Eckhart Tolle

You must be wondering, "I have a Strategic Objective. That is all well and good. But, Domenic, how do I translate this into a workable agenda to achieve this dream?"

Organizational Charts visually represent how your *future* business will look, feel, and be. It is a way of structuring your departments and team so that the company produces the results you've laid out within your Strategic Objective.

Let's examine how to start with your Strategic Objective and build solid, visual Organizational Charts.

Let's take the organization I collaborated with from the previous chapters: the BEST Landscape and Snow Company.

In the following tables, 2014 (Present) is taken from our end-of-year sales and our team.

Step back in time with me to 2014: $1 million in gross sales, 8 percent net profit, one salesperson, three foremen/nine crew members, three trucks, truck/office equipment, etc.

Our Strategic Objective 2019: $3 million in gross sales, 20 percent net profit, one manager/five salespeople, one supervisor/eight foremen/twenty-four crew members, eight trucks, truck/office equipment, etc.

To learn more about a Strategic Objective Template, click here or put the link in your browser for bonus material on my website: TomatoPasteLeadership.com/bonus.

Let's take one part, Sales, to start:

	2014 (Present)	2015	2016	2017	2018	2019
Sales	$1m	$1.25m	$1.5m	$1.75m	$2.25m	$3m
Sales Personnel	1	2	3	3	4	4+2

When we wrote their first Strategic Objective, sales were run by one person, selling $1 million of work.

Like so many companies, the owner was only a salesperson, and they were a super salesperson. When hiring other salespeople in the landscaping industry, you can expect fewer sales for those new sales hires. Let's use $500,000 sales per salesperson as a more reasonable sales goal.

For $1 million, we needed two people. For $1.5 million, we needed three salespeople. And so on.

We wanted the owner-salesperson to become a sales manager by 2019. His role would be strategic management as the team marketed and nurtured clients, mentored employees, and created tools for a $3 million-plus company.

The company would also need an assistant to manage and track the estimates, proposals, and contract paperwork at that stage.

The new sales manager and administrative assistant roles represent the other employees of the +2.

Let's look at another section, the Production of the Strategic Objective:

	2014 (Present)	2015	2016	2017	2018	2019
Sales	$1m	$1.25m	$1.5m	$1.75m	$2.25m	$3m
Production Personnel	9	12	15	18	26+1	36+2

The same thing needed to happen in production. With $1 million in gross sales, serving the clients' requests required three crews, each consisting of a foreman and two workers. We knew that each crew produced approximately $300,000 of work sold, which was our baseline.

Our first Strategic Objective was a substantial 30 percent growth yearly for $1 million in 2019. We knew from our plan that we would need four crews to serve that level of sales.

Notice the +1 in 2018 and the +2 in 2019. When six to eight crews are running the following year, a supervisor (+1) and a production assistant (+2) are needed.

Another area is the accounting department:

	2014 (Present)	2015	2016	2017	2018	2019
Sale	$1m	$1.25m	$1.5m	$1.75m	$2.25m	$3m
Accounting Personnel	0	0	1	1	2	2

I find in many clients that the owner or owner's spouse controls this area in many companies. I know how hard it is to give up this area. I agree there are many concerns with safety, security, employee pay, financials, etc.

There are solutions to the concerns, but you will need help managing the paperwork for a $2 million company. Strategically, again, we needed to hire one office staff member within two years, and in another two years, we would need one more. The total office staff by 2018 had to include two admins, with one manager managing them and working.

We will examine one more area: Equipment Needs: From 2014 to the final year of the Strategic Objective, we had to buy one truck with equipment annually to meet our sales and production goals.

One advantage of knowing your future needs is that you can make quick decisions when any resource becomes available or comes across your proverbial desk. Now, because we knew our long-term needs, when something came into our preview, we could make better, faster choices when those resources or deals popped up.

It is that old story of looking to buy a yellow VW Bug. Once you know you will be purchasing one, yellow VW Bugs seem to be everywhere.

Another resource that became readily available in this industry, as I assume in many other sectors, is that you can always find deals when someone leaves a business. I found this resource when I grew my organization and the many industries I coach. Companies always seem to be downsizing or no longer in business. I often picked up trucks and equipment this way.

Charting Your Future

Let's turn these numbers and statistics into Organizational Charts that satisfy our Strategic Objective.

Sales Organizational Chart

You will need one manager, five salespeople, one supervisor, eight foremen, and twenty-four crew members to run your future company. For shits and giggles, I also want to have one assistant in each department. We will continue building out these roles' responsibilities in the coming chapters. For now, it's enough to name them:

- Manager

- Administrative Assistant

- Salesperson

Service/Production Organizational Chart

- Manager
- Administrative Assistant
- Supervisor
- Foreman
- Crew

Accounting Organizational Chart

- Manager

- Administrative Assistant

- Accounts Payable

- Accounts Receivable

- Payroll.

Having well-conceived Organizational Charts allows everyone to see how the strategy will come to life. It is not just the who, what, when, and where but precisely who will make it happen. Then, the leaders can focus on mentoring and managing with more transparent communication. They know who is accountable for what role and how each role affects others, and they can nurture each of those individuals to thrive in their role.

There is more for each team member with the Organizational Charts than their tasks and responsibilities. Each employee has a straightforward view of where everyone in the organization stands and what they are responsible for. They also can see from the charts what future opportunities they have. By having more opportunities for your employees, you, as a leader, have created a reassuring sense of clarity and stability that few other systems or structures can develop.

This is the power of an Organizational Chart!

Now, let's look at what happens when we begin integrating it.

To learn more about an Organizational Chart template, click here or put the link to my website's bonus material in your browser: TomatoPasteLeadership.com/bonus.

CHAPTER 11:
The Circular Organizational Chart

"You cannot save people. You can only love them."

—Anaïs Nin

My partner and I had trained our workers to depend on us for everything. We would give them the schedule, help load the trucks in the mornings, ensure all the materials were on the trucks, meet the crews on the job to provide directions, and train them not to make decisions independently.

Consultants told us we should give the foremen more power, but we were afraid they would not do things the way we owners would. It was our money on the line, our livelihood, so we took it as our responsibility to do everything.

We had a bunch of good workers, but they were only followers. You can't blame them! They were following our glorified worker-owner management example.

Even if we had known how to let go of some of that responsibility, the workers' job descriptions were not defined enough to give them any autonomy.

An Organizational Chart identifies the roles or positions of the networks of people contributing to your organization. The network comes in many forms: employees, subcontractors, professionals, and vendors.

These are the people who run the systems that run your company.

These are the people who share your values and culture.

These are the people you mentor to the culture and toward the vision.

The people who help you and your company grow and sustain success.

It's time to see them a little more clearly.

The Network Effect

Systems run the company, but it flows when the employees are connected in their respective departments, and each department is connected to the other departments.

The sales department is connected to the accounting department, the production department to the accounting and sales departments, and the accounting department to sales.

This connection may seem like a simple idea. You may even say, "Hey, Domenic, doesn't every company have this down already?"

The simple answer is a big fat no!

Early on, the owner seems like the glue that holds everything together. The owner manages everything: sales, service, production, and accounting. This type of glue is a facade.

When a business grows into multiple departments, the owner does not have enough glue—or time—to be everywhere. The facade, the glue, or the owner comes apart at the seams, even though we often try to keep this connection.

"Treat every employee, every subcontractor, and every department as you would a client."

—Domenic A Chiarella

The glue inside all great and growing organizations is *understanding* and *living* the value that each employee treats everyone like a client. Each employee treats their team in a department as they treat a client, and each department treats all departments as they treat a client. It is a mindset.

An employee is not *just* performing a task. They also take care of the person behind and ahead of them in the company's workflow, and they should do so with the care they'd take when servicing a paying client.

A company is a whole living organism in which each and every part is essential.

I know how easy it is for one person to feel like the most critical part of an organization, and I understand how a department can believe it is the most essential part.

I'm reminded of this little story about the body:

The body parts argue over who should be in charge.

The brain says she should be in charge because she keeps everything running.

The blood thinks he should be in charge because he delivers oxygen to everything else.

The eyes say they should be in charge because they see where the body is going.

The stomach says she should be in charge because she provides energy.

Suddenly, the rectum speaks up and says he should be in charge because he is in charge of getting rid of waste.

They all laugh at the rectum and call him names.

Frustrated, the rectum shuts down and stops working.

Soon, the brain is hurting. The stomach is bloated. The blood is full of toxins.

So they give in and let the rectum be in charge.

Moral of the story: You do not always have to be smart to be in charge—just an asshole.

Departments are like body parts. Like the body's interconnected systems, departments must work together seamlessly to achieve common goals and drive the company forward.

Treat Everyone Like a Client

How often have you heard someone say to someone in another department, "I am too busy for that," or "I have too many more important things that I am doing," or "Can I just get back to you?"

You would very rarely see that happening if a client asked for something. It is, "Yes, ma'am," or "Yes, sir. When do you need it? Let me stop the presses. You are the client. You are what we are here for."

What happens internally when we treat everyone like we treat clients?

Yes, a company needs sales to move forward. But how do you satisfy the client without delivering the sold service? When the project has to be started and completed, the production department is king of the hill. Without them, the work doesn't get done.

How about the invoicing department? The company doesn't get paid if the client doesn't get invoiced consistently and correctly in a timely fashion. So, who should be king now?

How about payroll? If employees are not paid right, the company stops on a dime.

The vendor payments? Well, I'm not sure you can do work without materials.

At any given time, one department is just as essential as another. Each department's vital role becomes the success of the whole organization, whether it's sales, production, accounting, or payroll. While one department may be king of the hill and take the spotlight at a particular time, collaboration ensures that the organization moves forward harmoniously toward its goals.

Otherwise, at any given time, the department is an... (am I afraid to say this? See the above moral of the body story for the answer.)

This perspective on teamwork, collaboration, and interconnectedness is not new. I am sure you understand what a traditional Organizational Chart looks like and how it works. You have heard it all before.

The difference is how you see your role and the department role listed on the chart and how all the roles and departments treat each other.

The importance of treating every individual within the organization, whether employee, subcontractor, or department, with the same level of care and attention as a valued client, cannot be just words on the wall like a Ben & Jerry's. Adopting a client-centric mindset (where everyone is treated like a client) cultivates a culture of respect, collaboration, and excellence.

The leader's inspiration to cultivate this culture of values, empowerment, connection, and mutual respect will ultimately lead to greater success and fulfillment for employees and the company. This culture is part of the secret to creating a thriving organization.

CHAPTER 12:
Charting the Vision

"The way a team plays as a whole determines its success. You may have the greatest bunch of individual stars in the world, but if they don't play together, the club won't be worth a dime."

—Babe Ruth

After we work on Purpose in Life and create a new Strategic Objective in a coaching scenario, the owners often begin their Organizational Chart by naming people-oriented jobs rather than position-oriented ones.

Here is what I mean.

Rose is in the office. Her functions are invoicing, payroll, truck tire ordering, material ordering, and chief bottle washer (another of Dad's quotes.) So when we need more help in the office, let's hire another Rose!

Antonio is a great foreman. He creates and manages all the work orders, cleans the office and trucks, makes sales, and does some hiring. We need five more foreman positions; let's create more Antonios!

Mary does the material ordering, insurance, sales filing, and accounts payable. She also signs the payroll checks *and cleans the toilets* (Dad again).

There has to be a Mary position in the Org Chart!

My question is simple: how on earth do you duplicate a Mary? An Antonio? A Rose? What are their titles? How do you advertise for a job like that?

Can you imagine that job search?

All-Around Rose position needed. We are looking for a bright, hardworking person, a payroll specialist, accounts payable, production material handler, production scheduler, insurance specialist, and chief bottle washer. Please call Mary (because she is the new go-to HR employee hirer)!

If Mary wants to move up that Organizational Chart to become a Rose, how do we replace Mary? How do we compensate Mary, now a Rose? How can she move to a better or higher position when she seems irreplaceable where she is?

A healthier approach to creating these charts is to create result-oriented titles for each position. Remember that each position in each department in the company's Organizational Chart must satisfy the Strategic Objective.

Then, we can find people to fill those positions.

Think of a football team. You have different coaches: head, offensive, defensive, etc. You have a team composed of quarterbacks, running backs, offensive lines, and defensive lines (a Complete Football Organizational Chart). Each position has a common goal of achieving success in winning a Super Bowl (a Strategic Objective). Each position has one result to achieve (running backs run the ball while the offensive line protects the quarterback and running backs).

Suppose one player, such as a defensive lineman (position), gets hurt or is tired. In that case, you can easily replace that player with another defensive lineman.

If your defensive coach is not producing good results, you may be looking for a new one.

When you are developing a better team to create that Super Bowl result, one look at your Organizational Chart may show you that you lack defensive positions. Now, you will focus more on what you need and how you will train, and your people will know exactly what to focus on.

You can hire and train for that position while developing a team to grow to a $3 million (Super Bowl) result. You lack production foreman positions, not Antonio positions.

The key to an Organizational Chart is to keep it position-oriented, not people-oriented.

The Rubber Hits the Road

Setting up a new Organizational Chart in this manner is hard work. It is hard to spell out the results each role requires, as well as the strategic responsibilities and the tactical work. This is tedious stuff. It's just as tricky keeping track of all those hats or hoping you'll hire the right person by luck or magic.

I ran into this with an owner and her partner in Florida after a keynote speech on the art of delegation.

After any speech or keynote, many owners come up to the front of the stage. Some compliment me (this warms my heart), and some ask more questions (I enjoy their enthusiasm). Yet, there is always so much noise as the audience leaves the auditorium. I do my best to focus on each person and listen closely. I give them enough time to answer thoroughly or present them with a potential direction.

An hour before my next engagement, I was headed to a round-table lunch—my favorite thing to do at these conferences—when two owners caught me and asked for a moment. I said, "For the price of a good cup of coffee, I can help."

Maria introduced herself and her brother, Marco. They said they were having problems with timely invoice processing. One storm event would take her accounting department two weeks to complete the paperwork and send invoices to the clients.

Maria managed and worked in accounting, while Marco was in sales and production. Marco told me that snow events could come one after another. Maria told me that two people took two full weeks to process each event, so that was two weeks for each event plus the overlap—a chaotic process if this happened.

For the life of them, they couldn't figure out how to fix it.

We had a great chat discussing key elements. I put some system flows, processes, and templates on the whiteboard for Maria to take photos. They took some good ideas home and planned to start working on the process.

A few weeks later, Maria called to ask if I would take on the invoicing project. They'd had four snow events within two weeks and were out of control. The accounting employees were overworked and frustrated. The work was getting impossible, and the clients were not getting their invoices. Her voice shook with frustration.

I agreed to the project.

First, I needed to diagnose the issues. The owners explained what they thought the problem was, but I needed to understand it from every angle. After the owner meeting, we sat down with everyone who touched the invoice to complete the diagnosis part of the project.

We started by looking at the people and their jobs in each department, the systems running each department, and how the company was interconnected. The goal was to sketch a flow process of the invoicing working backward (I love starting with the end in mind) from an effective outcome to the work orders, the sales contract, etc.

First, we asked the following questions:

- **Accounting:**
    - How were the clients invoiced?
    - How did work orders come into the department, and how were they managed and filed?

- **Production:**
    - o How were work orders verified and approved?
    - o How were work orders completed?
- **Sales:**
    - o How were work orders prepared from sales?
    - o How were they selling work?

For each question, we asked the same follow-up: who did the work?

To fix the invoicing issue in the accounting department, we had to resolve the problems with the work orders and how they were filed. We then had to look at how the work orders flowed from the production department.

To fix the issues in production, we had to fix the work order completions and verification. We then had to look at how the work orders were created and sent to them from sales.

To fix the issues in sales, I found that we had to fix how the contracts were turned into work orders and how they were sent to production. Holy shit!

One glaring issue was that they didn't know who was doing what work in any of the three departments. *Hmm, that seems like an Organizational Chart and Position issue.* Like many small businesses, everyone wore many hats that would cut across many departments.

Maria invoiced and sold contracts, performed payroll, dispatched, and assisted with work orders. If I had looked hard enough, I am sure she would have been cleaning the bathrooms! Everyone did everything.

To add insult to injury, Maria and Marco wanted to hire more salespeople.

You know the old saying that a picture is worth a thousand words? I showed them the complete picture of their organization to make my answer easy to understand and to help them see how to solve the issues.

I mapped out a 30,000-foot project for Maria and Marco to fix their two-week-per-snow-event invoicing issue. I explained that we had to start in sales, then move to production, and finally correct the problem in accounting.

I showed them the company's Organizational Chart, positions, systems, flows, and templates.

Now, we needed to refine the project. Maria and Marco could not believe the scope of solving the invoice issue. Much to their dismay, I was going to start in sales. Before I laid out the whole process, Marco said, "Dom, WTF are you doing in the sales department? We are having an invoice issue."

Let me take just one area of the expanded project.

There were three salespeople in the department. They performed many sales tasks: taking calls, making proposals, running estimates, tracking, and closing sales duties. You name the task, and each salesperson does it. So, of course, they needed more salespeople, right? They thought their problem was work overload. The salespeople could not take on more work, which meant they needed more people.

Ahh, the many-hats syndrome. (I wonder where we've seen that before.)

I started by removing each person's hats and assigning them to a single position in the Sales Organizational Chart. Each position was given a definitive result, a position to report to, any positions who reported to them, the strategic work they were to perform in the larger workflow, and the tactical tasks that would lead to their position's result.

I showed Maria, Marco, and the Sales Department that tools like a Sales Organization Chart and Positions can transform many-hat syndrome into three existing position-oriented salespeople with focused results and without unnecessary paperwork. This would save 50 percent of their time, adding two people's worth of work without hiring anyone else.

They had thought throwing warm salespeople's bodies at the department would fix their problems. However, the issues were foundational and structural problems in the company. We built a clear Sales Organizational Chart and filled it with people-oriented positions, and the magic happened.

Was it a tedious process? Yes. Was the work worth it? You tell me.

Great leaders guide great employees who are willing to do something new, which leads to more sales, the ability to serve more clients, and more profits in less time. Of course, all of them were alongside a solid coach. LOL.

Sales went from $2 million to $5 million in less than two seasons.

More importantly, employees were more effective, happier, and thriving in the new environment.

STEP 1:
Conclusion

"Leading is a skill, not a gift. You're not born with it; you learn how."

—Seth Godin

For the final two years of my dad's life, I had the honor of being his partner on his journey toward the next chapter.

I have no regrets about putting my coaching business on the back burner. Family has always been one of my most important values and purposes. Though it may seem strange to say, those final years with my dad—despite his passing—were a beautiful time and a true highlight of our relationship.

We had a conversation I will never forget on a drive home from a doctor's appointment. I remember exactly where I was on the road—off exit twenty-five, a ramp in Waterbury, Connecticut.

Dad had had heart issues for quite some time, and his doctor was considering aorta valve surgery. After a battery of tireless tests, Dad turned to me and said, "Boy, am I relieved to find out that I don't have to have heart surgery. I wouldn't have made it out of surgery this time, Domenic. I am sure it would have killed me. Thank god it was only my weak heart."

It caught me off guard, and I had to look at Dad to see what he was thinking. He was relieved that it was only a bad heart, not surgery. Dad was a straight shooter. He knew his limitations.

I looked over as I was downshifting off the exit and saw he was deep in thought.

He turned to me again and said, "You know, Domenic, something that has been on my mind for some time...I am sorry that I wasn't a smarter businessman. I chose to buy an electronics firm many years ago. I thought it would be more than it was. I took a financial hit and found that I bought something that was an extremely less profitable business. If I'd stayed with Hewlett-Packard, I could have given you and the family much more."

I knew what he was talking about. You see, he had worked with David Packard of Hewlett-Packard in the early days of computers. At the beginning of this new field, Dad was right there, making four or five times what most middle-class people were making. He missed out on the computer wave and, apparently more importantly, the financial wealth it would have brought by buying an electronics firm instead of staying with HP.

He softly continued, "I could have made so much more money. I could have given you and Anna and your brothers so much more in life."

I was shocked. Dad had made innocuous comments like this before, but I didn't think much of them. I could not believe that Dad had harbored this with so much pain all these years.

It was an emotional moment for both of us.

I composed myself and said, "Dad, you may not have realized this, but you gave me so much more than money. Growing up in your business gave me invaluable business mentoring and real-life experience. Very few people have that opportunity. For me, it was like a six-year internship, and then afterward, we partnered up to make it a multimillion-dollar venture."

I continued, "Because of your choice, I learned all the basics and foundations of the business. Where on earth can you get that? Because of your time with me, not your money, I was able to take that experience and build my landscape/snow business to the top 3 percent in North America. I could never have done that if you had only given me money."

I waited for that to sink in and then continued, "You know that having a lot of money would not have made me the businessman, the father, and the man I am today. Money would have bought me fast cars and nuttier friends in the crazy 1970s. I would have killed myself being rich without earning it. I was much better off, and I had to work hard for what I needed in life. No, Dad. I am proud and happy to have been part of your life and business. Thank you."

The truth is simple: time is much more limited than money. I am grateful for the success skills I learned from my dad. I am thankful to have been blessed by my Italian grandparents, who did not have money but gave my parents and us something more substantial. I am grateful to have been wired for high achievement and given a way to be okay with failure and success.

I am grateful that someone has been watching over me all these years. Maybe my Nonna, the matriarch, was still watching over me. She immigrated here from Italy with two nickels to rub together. God has blessed me with inspiration and the ability to understand this experience and knowledge. My family helped me keep my options open and make decisions. They helped me change course or double down as opportunities arose.

These generationally passed-down values have translated into my purposes. My purposes filtered into the culture of my organization, which grew to a level that allowed me to reach the kind of success I'd once dreamed about—the kind that allowed me to be there for my family.

For the last year and a half of his life, my dad lived in an assisted living facility with twenty-four-hour surveillance to ensure he was okay and eating correctly. My wife, my daughters, and I spent much of our time with him there—almost every single day. Most of my afternoons and dinners were with him.

It was among the happiest times I ever spent with my dad. Part of the reason was that I could put my business on the back burner to be there for him.

I say back burner because was it luck that I had that time free? Was I so financially secure that I could take the time? Did I have people in positions to do the work when I needed it?

Those factors all played a part. More importantly, I set up my business to satisfy my Purposes in Life, including family time. I built a team with my values, culture, and strategy that could run things even if I couldn't be there.

I spent my resources in business and at home without over-extending either. I had time to do things with my family. I had time to do things for my company, employees, and clients.

The ability to be there for those precious final days with my dad was not a stroke of luck or financial freedom—it was a consequence of conscious choices.

This is why success is not merely measured in profits but in the richness of relationships, the joy of shared moments, and the legacy we leave behind.

What legacy do you want to leave behind?

How will your relationships and actions shape that legacy?

What does success mean to you, and is it reflected in your values?

Do you want to set up your business and life so that you can do the things that matter most to you?

My final words for this first section of your journey are a reminder that your transformation will not be a straightforward process; it will require dedication, hard work, and purpose. It will require you to make choices.

While addressing issues with systems (Step 3) and people (Step 2) will be crucial, the true linchpin of an organization's growth lies in the leader's development—the foundation we've laid here in Step 1.

What's the heart of this development you're pursuing? Why does your organization exist? What are its values? What's its mission? These are more than questions. The answers are the way of life that you and every member of your team are creating. It is a story you use that will reinforce every departmental strategy, every operational detail, and every customer experience. That's what it means to have a company strategy and a mission.

Then, the path to success is paved with a commitment to leadership development, shared values, a clear vision, and a plan to achieve it.

As we close this section and move on to the next, remember that the path to success begins with you. Embrace your values, define your vision, and lead with purpose.

Your journey awaits.

STEP 2:
Developing Your Employees

"Before you become a leader, success is all about growing your-self. After you become a leader, success is about growing others."

—Jack Welch, CEO of General Electric

In the first section, Tomato Paste Leadership was about un-covering your purpose—who you are and why you exist—and growing to become a better leader. Now, let's get down to un-covering your business purpose.

Before we start, I want you to take a leap of faith with me. I want you to consider your company's growth and prosperity from a different point of view: the employee's perspective.

Employee Development is the second step of our three key principles. These are the people who run your company. They invest much of their time, energy, passion, and lives into mak-ing your business thrive. A leader recognizes their pivotal role in providing a return on that investment—in more than just a paycheck.

Leaders recognize employees as an extension of themselves, representing their business and serving their clients.

How do you reciprocate their dedication? Well, money is cer-tainly one thing. But here, we're going to look at three things you might not have considered:

1. An opportunity to work in an environment aligned with their values and in a role where they can thrive.
2. Orientation and a warm welcome into the environment.

3. Continued opportunities for growth, development, and investments in their future.

These are the ingredients to come. Don't worry—I'll also help you put them together.

INGREDIENT 4:
Hiring to Values

"With the right people, culture, and values, you can accomplish great things."

—Tricia Griffith

In the preface, I brought you to a team meeting before the Snowstorm of the Century. Maybe you can still envision the sparkle in Julio's eyes as he invited me in, or perhaps you can laugh with me at Mina's "Go do something else, Domenic" musings.

In that meeting, I witnessed my company rise to a new level. My employees worked as a team, each thriving in their role and knowing they were an essential part of the organization.

I marveled at their success as it became mine.

That meeting inspired me to be and do more of what I was leading us toward. My investment in them paid off in spades, with the company's growth, their growth, and, finally, my freedom.

I remember thinking, *I'm on the right track. Holy shit, I am part of this team!* Nothing energizes an owner more than seeing this transformation come to life. I had created this environment for them, and they excelled in it.

Yet the question of all the questions someone growing their company will ask me is, "Domenic, where can I find great employees like Julio and Mina?"

How did my employees become superstars?

How did they take such owner-like actions?

How did I unearth that hidden potential in my team?

What is the secret ingredient?

Let me ask you this: how often do we ask what great employees are looking for in *us*?

Simple, huh? Humor me just for a few minutes.

Let's first look at the tools you use to lead your organization and run your business.

Your Strategic Objective gives potential employees a clear picture of your organization's direction. It is the who, what, where, and when of who you are.

The company's Organizational Chart lets them see where their position fits and what future positions may be available.

When you hire by a Position Agreement (more on this in a moment) for each role within the Organizational Chart, they have clear responsibilities to fulfill instead of navigating the "many hats" approach they'd find in most organizations.

Something surprising happens: they see who you are with your Company Values. Initially, a potential employee can only read about this culture. Only time will tell working at your organization whether what you write and say is what you believe in and how you truly live.

When your Company Values are honest, accurate, and lived, it's the tool that will help you find the best potential employee. When someone who shares your values steps into a clear and aligned role for themselves, you have the chance to create art.

Hire for values first and skills second.

To be clear, hiring someone who fits the kind of culture you are working to build and showing them how to participate in it will not save time upfront. In the short term of growing your business, you must slow down to get this right. You will have to do double duty with the worker-owner in you and your transformation as a leader and mentor. Your patience and kindness must be on display.

The good news is that a team with similar values and culture will be unstoppable in the long term.

Key Concepts

- **Foundational Values:** While skills can be developed and learned, values serve as the bedrock of your organization. Hiring employees who align with your company's values ensures a cohesive and purpose-driven workforce. Skills can be developed, but values are foundational.

- **A Collective Mind:** You don't have to have the best individual thinking; you must have team thinking. It is not the most intelligent, experienced employees who make a team. It is a collection of minds and focused individuals. You will be unstoppable.

- **Craft Clarity:** Position Agreements are crucial documents that outline the roles, responsibilities, and resources associated with a particular role within the organization. This clarity sets the stage for a successful employment relationship. Clarity brings understanding.

- **Put Down the Hats:** Positions define the challenges of integrating employees with complicated roles into your new organizational structures. I'll teach you a seamless method for incorporating these versatile employees into your new organizational charts and thriving work environment.

CHAPTER 13:
Values First

"If you pick the right people and give them the opportunity to spread their wings, and put compensation as a carrier behind it, you almost don't have to manage them."

—Jack Welch

One of my favorite parts of attending business conferences is when they have roundtable lunches. You can shoot the business shit and enjoy a hot lunch all at once.

These tables are always full of owners ready to learn the keys to everyday issues.

The Snow Association Conferences had lunch setups, and I loved to volunteer as a table moderator. I always looked for opportunities to do as much damage—I mean mentoring—as possible in our forty-five-minute break.

I remember attending one in Louisville in the summer of 2019, right before COVID-19 closed the world down when I chose the "employee development" table.

As we were munching away, we introduced ourselves and started discussing our employee issues.

I knew what would come out of everyone's mouth. One owner after another said the same thing:

"I can't find good employees."

"If I can find them, I can't keep them for long."

"I give them so much, yet they still leave."

Round and round the table it goes. Where will it stop? Nobody knows.

One of the owners asked me, "What do you think is the key to making people come to the table? How do we get them to do what we want?"

I said, "I do not believe you can make anyone come to the table. You cannot make anyone do anything."

Chirp, chirp, chirp. (Those crickets like to follow me around.)

I continued, "What if we look at it from their point of view? What would I be looking for in your company if I were looking for a job?"

I believe if I were a would-be employee, I would want some of these things:

- To be successful in life.

- To be in a career that would respect what I do for their company.

- To give my job 100 percent and to be rewarded financially for it.

- To be in a place where I can become more of a professional and know I have future opportunities.

The answers to all the owners' questions at the roundtable and anyone who wants to grow their company come *from the employees* and how desirable you are *to them*.

If you want to hire employees who share your values, you have to put your values first.

Your Challenge: Should You Accept It

For all the ways we might grow or find more profits, none of them can happen without great employees. But I'll repeat it: I do not believe you can make anyone come to the table. You cannot make anyone do anything.

If I were a potential employee of your company, what would I have to see to make me want to work there?

Are the values of the company and what you preach the values you live by?

Could I be successful in the organization?

Where is the company going in the future?

Would I fit into the organization if I joined it?

Before asking why employees are hard to find, we need to ask why they would want to work for us and ensure we are set up to hire and develop them if they do.

As the leader, you know what you want from life—your Purpose in Life.

You know where you want your company to go   your Strategic Objective.

Now you can see the company taking shape around that vision—an Organizational Chart.

To find people who want to step into the roles that will bring the Strategic Objective to life, you must share your inspiration with them. Values are a pathway to leadership, self- or team management, creativity, and growth for them just as much as they are for you.

Sharing the organization's values motivates them to show up daily, ready to take on a new challenge as the company's mission advances.

Back at the Snow Convention roundtable, the other owners were still puzzled, looking for the magic pill that would "help" these motivated, owner-like employees to the table.

One asked, "Domenic, you had great employees. How on earth did they work and act like owners?"

I told him that I hired them to be part of my values and, most importantly, that they had to be teachable, be ready to learn, and share the value of being part of a system and a team.

I was not hiring people to build rocket ships or perform brain surgery. If I were, I would undoubtedly hire for skills. I was looking for a company fit. Being a good fit and having shared values were more important than any skills they might have.

I don't want to mislead you. I understand how much work it is to hire the right people, train them, and develop them. Let me tell you, it is nothing compared to hiring, firing, and redoing the process over and over. It takes a lot of time and, indeed, a lot of money to keep a workforce in place.

Most people hire someone from their resume. You have a position to fill. Someone applies. You look at their resume. *OMG, what a beautiful bunch of skills.* Voila, you have a winner.

At first, I filled my ranks this way. It always seemed I needed employees quickly, and a resume gave me an idea of their unbelievable skills and experience. Sometimes, I found a great employee that way.

Most times, I failed to find the *right* employee.

Finding someone who fits into the organization, even if they still have skills to learn, is more challenging than just looking at resumes. But it is much more reliable on the other side.

Let's revisit the last chapters to see what tools you have available during the hiring stage:

- Your one-page Strategic Objective informs you of the company's who, what, when, and where. It helps give potential employees a map to understand what the company does, its operations, where it is going, and its future.

- Your Company Values, based on your Purpose in Life, will guide you in the questions you ask during an interview. They are also the starting point for potential employees to read about the company's culture.

- The Organizational Chart includes the positions you must fill and the agreements required. These charts show who's who in the organization. They make the potential employee's position transparent regarding the results you expect from them. They allow the employees to know they are responsible for those results instead of just accomplishing a list of tasks.

- The Position Agreement is a job description on steroids. More on this later in this chapter.

Put together a packet of each document above in print or PDF/presentation form. You and your potential employee discuss these areas in the interview. You can talk about the company, the position, the future, and life—not just their background and skills.

Interviewing to Values

Interviews are stressful enough without adding interrogation to the atmosphere. Set up the meeting to get acquainted and try to put the person at ease.

One great way to start the meeting is to ask what the potential employee is passionate about. I don't care if it is bird watching.

I want to see the energy in their mannerisms and sparkle in their eyes as they tell you about birds and their mating rituals. (Where do you think I learned why woodpeckers peck the wood shingles on my house in the spring?)

Leading, yes-no questions don't tell you anything. "Do you work well in a team? Do you have our values? Do you work hard? Are you teachable?" Of course, the answer would be yes. "You're hired!"

Instead, look for a fit through their values. Knowing that one of our values was education and that I was looking for a teachable person, I would ask, "What kind of education have you accomplished lately? What books are you reading?" If they didn't read books or go to classes, chances are they would not be learners and would not thrive in our organization.

For the value of systems, I looked for people who valued being part of a team.

"Tell me about your best project. How did you handle it?" Did they take credit for everything they achieved? How did they work with others to get the job done?

"Tell me about your worst project. How did you handle it?" Did they take control and order everyone around? Did they micromanage from that point on?

As they answered in detail, I listened carefully and could tell much more accurately whether they were team players than if I had asked them outright, and they knew I wanted them to say yes.

I do not know all the dos and don'ts one can discuss during an interview. Please look at the laws in your area. I know that I can always share about my life, my family, my aspirations, how the company started, and my work situations. If they so choose, they can reciprocate. Like meeting someone new, I am interested in learning about them and what matters to them.

I also know there are no right or wrong people, no good or bad people. If we do not hire someone, it is not that they are a bad or a wrong person. It has nothing to do with good or bad. We look for and hire people who are the right fit for the company and our values.

An example of a bad fit is if someone is not a learner. They will be a bad fit. They will find it hard to learn new systems and flow.

Someone with a lone wolf personality is not wrong or bad, either. However, they will find it hard to be part of a team. The current employees depend on each other. This is another thing that this employee would find challenging.

A good-fit employee will be happy in my environment.

As a leader, one of my responsibilities is finding people who share my values and are great fits.

An unhappy employee leads to an unhappy team, which leads to unhappy clients. Unhappy clients make for a very unhappy owner. Don't forget my family. My daughters were very unhappy while we were on vacation.

Another part of the interview is looking for *potential*. Your potential in life and business is not how high you reach but how far you climb to get there. You can't tell where people will land from where they begin. With the right opportunity and motivation to learn, anyone can build the skills to achieve extraordinary things. Your potential is not a matter of where you start but how far you travel. Focus less on starting points and more on distance traveled.

I once was looking for a new employee for a sales position. The potential employee, Ron, was choosing between two great companies.

During one of the interviews, he brought his wife with him to get her input.

Days later, he chose us.

One day during the orientation period, I asked him why he chose us.

He said, "Domenic, my wife and I were driving back home after the third interview. My wife told me I should choose your company over another great organization. She told me something hit her: It may be a better place to work."

I asked, "How did your wife arrive at that conclusion?"

Ron chuckled and said, "She had to use the restroom while we were talking. She found the bathroom was spotless and smelled great. She said that it was just an ordinary day. If they put this much care into a simple thing like a spotless, great-smelling bathroom, they do everything else that way."

Well, who knew our value of "image" would find us a great employee in an unexpected, totally welcoming way?

Leadership Through Hiring

Monkeys can be taught skills, and computers and robots can be programmed to do skills. However, what makes us human is our values and character.

The leader you are becoming continues to take shape in this hiring and development arena.

You are not just acquiring knowledge about hiring. You are building character as a leader.

You are not just trying to understand a process of recognizing, correcting, and preventing mistakes. You are also (OMG, am I saying this?) striving to *increase* mistakes so that you can improve your learning.

You learn so much faster when you make mistakes. Encouraging yourself and your employees to make more mistakes will result in fewer mistakes. Each mistake helps you remember the right way.

The most significant part of my mentoring and coaching is praising people for trying.

I used to teach many people, friends, and my family how to ski. It was a struggle. Downhill skiing is a challenging sport to learn and master. When we struggled to get down a particularly steep and bumpy hill, I would love to stop after completing a difficult section where we just struggled.

I would ask, "How was that?"

I would listen to their struggles and how they made many mistakes.

Then, after listening, I would say, "Stop for a second. Turn around. Look up the hill. That is what you accomplished. That is what you just did."

Their response was always, "Holy cow. I did that?"

Yes, you did!

Like stopping, turning, and looking up the ski slope, I also helped my employees see what they were pulled toward doing more of instead of pushing themselves through struggles.

If you wait until you have all the knowledge, you may never start to learn or pursue your dreams. You may know more or have more knowledge. You may never be fully prepared. You damn well become prepared when you leap anyway.

Hire someone with most of your values and who is ready to take a leap, even if it means you may make some hiring mistakes that will happen along the way.

On his first day, he marveled at our wall of front-page magazines. We were on the pages of quite a few industry magazines. He said, "You must be proud of the front pages. Wow, what achievements. I wonder what other companies think about how you are on top."

I thought about it for a few seconds. Then I pointed to one magazine. "You know, Ken, that magazine was three years ago. That one was last year. Sure, we are proud of our accomplishments. Yet these are from the past. This is a new year. We are not competing with another company but with our future selves. We strive to improve, learn more, and find better ways to grow."

Ken looked at me and said, "Then I am in the right place—a place to improve. To grow."

That is who you want to hire.

CHAPTER 14:
Hire to Positions

"Build your own dreams, or someone else will hire you to build theirs."

—Farrah Gray

One sunny Friday morning, I was in my office working on last-minute paperwork before heading out to take care of my top client. I was looking forward to a great weekend filled with family events and, if I found the extra time (and I usually did), a bit of system development.

Around the shop, the Friday energy was palpable—it was payday!

In the early days, we paid our employees on Thursdays. Our old workforce didn't like to come to work on Fridays. It wasn't that they were bad people; they were hard workers who had different priorities. Payday Thursdays turned into Party Thursday Nights and No-Show Fridays.

The solution? Pay the employees on Friday and finish the week's work *before* the celebrations begin. So, Payday Fridays became the standard.

One of the production men knocked at my office door on this particular Friday. He said, "Jefe, no cheque."

I thought the checks might be late and suggested he wait a little while.

But in a little while, another worker had the same issue.

Before I knew it, the "Jefe, no cheque" complaint had become a chorus.

I dropped what I was doing and told them, "Déjame ver qué pasó."

Let me see what happened.

I asked our payroll person, "Maggie, excuse me, do you have a moment?" I relayed their concerns, and she jumped right up with a response.

"Domenic, I am sorry. I did not get a chance to print the checks and get them in the envelopes. I did everything else, but I will stop what I am doing and get the checks out right now."

As I was leaving to update the employees, she added, "I know how you love systems, and this system we just created for payroll works. I did all the system steps except the last two: print the checks and distribute them to the production manager. You have to give me credit for doing most of them—ten out of twelve steps is pretty good, right?"

I was dumbfounded. I am sure I looked like it, too, with the head-cocked look a dog gives you when you ask it to go for a walk.

I thought, *Payroll is not done. The workers do not have their money. And she wants credit?*

Before I opened my mouth and said something stupid, I rubbed my head with both hands, took a breath, looked up, and chuckled.

She did have a crazy point, but a point nonetheless.

There *was* something wrong with this whole picture, but I couldn't put my dumbfounded finger on it. She did accomplish most of the tasks. I knew that I created this mess with her job. As she became more helpful and accomplished, I gave her more work. She followed my lead by wearing many hats.

She smiled back and said, "I'll get right on it, boss."

The Power of Position Agreements

Most organizations have task-oriented job descriptions. In Maggie's case, the twelve-step payroll task was part of her job. Other hats she wore included mail distribution, contract assistance, insurance, and a bit of this and a bit of that.

We were graduating to something new: building Position Agreements in our Organizational Charts. Position Agreements are job descriptions on steroids.

These are written, result-oriented agreements that clearly define an employee's responsibilities—for example, a task-oriented job description would be making sure the paychecks go out on Fridays. A result-oriented position would be to satisfy the employees.

When we created a Position Agreement for the payroll administrator role—a spot we'd created on our Accounting Organizational Chart—the results looked like this: "To effectively manage employee relationships, with responsibilities including recruiting, hiring, and ensuring competitive compensation, benefits, and effective training systems."

Yes, I said that with one breath.

Our focus needed to shift from asking her to juggle many tasks to trusting her to be responsible for "effective employee relationship management." The tasks were now tools to help her in her position, and the result of the position.

Doing most of the tasks (even ten out of twelve) did not produce the result of "managing employee relationships." This new approach made a huge difference and was a game changer in our organization and the many organizations I have coached.

The specifics of your Position Agreements should be tailored to your organization, but here are some essential components to include:

- **Position Name:** This should match a position on the Organizational Chart so that everyone knows where this position lies and what they do. A nice employee bonus is seeing what kind of mobility is available.

- **Who the Position Reports to and Who Reports to them:** This gives the employee a clear line through the chain of command. Someone somewhere in the company always thinks they can assign work to another person and tell them what to do. This stops misplaced commands in their tracks.

- **Results Statement:** This is one of the most critical parts of a Position Agreement. Employees who take on a position should have precise, measurable results for which they are responsible. This prevents the "Don't I get credit for ten out of twelve?" moments. (Who needs a payroll check, anyway?)

- **Strategic Component:** This is the higher-level work that the position will do for the company, such as mentoring staff, planning, developing systems, and fostering professional growth.

- **Tactical Component:** This section explains how the position will execute these tasks, systems, templates, methods, and flows. You have seen this section before; many companies call it a job description.

- **Company Standards:** These standards are the statements that guide the entire company. They summarize who you are and how you live, including your Company Values.

- **Signatures:** *The owner and employee complete the hiring session* by signing the entire position agreement.

Create a Position Agreement for each position on the Organizational Chart, with a wage attached. You'll now know what each position does, what results it is accountable for, and the pay range. You'll know who does what in the company, and so will everyone else.

Most importantly, each position will come with accountability, so a person doesn't just accept a job; they accept all its responsibilities. Wearing more than one hat (holding more than one position) is okay. However, to do so, they must satisfy the requirements of each position they agree to take on.

Position-Oriented vs. People-Oriented

I love Ray Dalio's analogy of a baseball team and a business—it is spot on:

> Imagine if you had baseball cards that showed all the performance stats for your people: batting averages, home runs, errors, ERAs, and win/loss records. You could see what they did well and poorly and call on the right people to play the right positions in a very transparent way.

This is an excellent picture of how Position Agreements can benefit your growing business. If you're not sure about the baseball parallels, let's recap:

- A Strategic Objective for a business might be to earn $3 million in five years; for a baseball team, it might be to win the World Series.

- Your Company Values indicate the values and culture of both business and baseball teams, as well as how a team acts and plays.

- An Organizational Chart for a business might include a president, salespeople, administrative staff, service personnel, etc. For baseball, it would include owners, managers, administrative staff, pitchers, catchers, etc.

Position Agreements round out this organizational clarity by defining the positions needed to achieve our goals—for business and baseball.

A baseball card shows the player's name, position, and performance statistics. These stats give a manager the tools to put the right player in the proper position to achieve the correct organizational result.

A baseball team also has many positions to fill—the first baseman, second baseman, pitcher, etc. When players are put into these positions, they know precisely what results they are responsible for producing.

However, this is one of the most critical parts of these agreements: an Organizational Chart and their positions are tailored to a team's objective, not to an existing individual's skills or interests.

Job descriptions quickly become summaries of the many hats one wears—a mishmash of tasks that a Maggie might do, often crossing various departments.

With a task-driven, people-oriented job description, an employee could have had the tasks of mail distribution, scheduling, payroll hour collection, payroll check distribution, work order creation, material ordering, vendor payments, assisting production, etc.—all gathered over time because of their interests or skills. Then, their job description would read as various headings with lists under each.

When hiring for a *position* within an Organizational Chart, you know exactly what you need to "win the World Series." And there is transparency for your players to know exactly what they're signing on to do.

CHAPTER 15:
Hire to Fit

The opportunity is not to discover the perfect company for ourselves. The opportunity is to build the perfect company for each other.

—Simon Sinek, *Find Your Why*

The transition from job descriptions to Position Agreements presents a fascinating dilemma. I am not trying to scare or stop you from taking this step. Hiring value-driven people for result-oriented Position Agreements is vital for growing and operating at the highest level.

The dilemma is the delicate task of guiding your existing employees into new positions.

I have learned, and I have coached this transition too many times. It can be very challenging for current employees. In my experience, many current employees do not, cannot, or will not make this transition.

There are many reasons: They are used to their old job descriptions. They have been wearing the many hats thrust upon them by the owners. Some of the employees might not like the results they are expected to achieve. Holding anyone responsible for issues is much more challenging when everyone does everything.

In my companies and the many I've coached, I've seen employees feel they were going backward with their titles. They had such long job descriptions before and now had just one responsibility. Was it a demotion? Sadly, hiring for values and positions exposes some of the employees. You will find that some employees have been hiding incompetence under their many hats.

I often find that employees who cannot or will not make this transition voluntarily leave the company, or you help them to another company.

Holding the Line

Hiring new employees doesn't involve reconditioning or transitioning. However, learning to hire did come with plenty of trials and tribulations for me.

David had previously worked as a consultant with our organization. He was a brilliant IPM (integrated pest management) specialist. He could examine a client's property, identify issues, recommend a solution, and then sell us pesticide products. We worked excellently together.

One day, he came to us looking for a career change. He wanted to leave his company and join our organization. Wow, an excellent salesman wanted to work for us! We made a sales position available. I hired him on the spot instead of working through our hiring-for-values process.

After a few months, employees in the sales department came to me concerned about how they had to do so many of David's tactical tasks.

Of course, in keeping with our value of "Systems Run the Company," there was our Sales Flow System. One process was the Estimate Process, which he was responsible for, and it flowed into the Proposal Process, for which another employee was responsible.

The flow went like this: a client would request a quote for a synthetic putting green. The sales admin would create a work order to estimate it and attach an estimate sheet to that work order. Having templates with the work order made it easy for the salesperson to quickly and consistently get the information from the field. Once they completed those forms, the salesperson would return their estimate to the sales admin. Then, she would use a specific calculation spreadsheet to quote the work and create a draft proposal. Once approved, the salesperson would get the proposal and do what they do best: close the deal. If we win the contract, it will be returned to the sales department to create the work orders, triggering another process in the sales department.

However, David did not consistently complete the estimate part of the template. Too often, the sales admin had to track him down to get the necessary information or data so she could complete the process of preparing the proposal.

I became aware of what was happening and focused on solving the chaos the situation caused in the department. I sat with David and discussed the systems, flows, templates, and people working with him. He understood, and off he went.

He failed to follow through on his part of the system many times, more than I would have liked. This noncompliance with systems and team issues kept popping up.

Two things could have resulted from this situation. I could have let the issue continue, especially since David was a great salesman. However, we must remember our value of "Service the Client, Period," including treating everyone like a client.

If I ignored David's behavior, I could not treat the sales admin like a client and give her what she needed. Covering for his behavior would mean doing more work and wearing David's and the sales admin's hats to ensure everything was done. That would work against my Purpose of having more free time with my family.

My leadership position was on display here.

My lack of leadership was displayed because I let this continue for too long. I could have become a better leader who led the other employees who ran the systems that ran the company.

This moment was when the rubber met the pavement, even if it meant admitting David wasn't a good fit.

David was a great guy. He didn't have any skills deficits or capability issues. However, I had not taken the time to see if he were a good fit for the results we needed from his role or the values he'd need to be part of the team. I wasn't yet mature enough to hire employees with our values, especially trainable ones who would work with systems, work with a team, and treat others in the company like clients.

All I had seen were his skills.

David was a lone wolf who didn't play well in the sandbox and liked to do things his way. He lacked our values of being on a team, learning, using systems, and respecting other positions that were part of those systems. He had the "sales is everything" mentality—and to be fair, his way of selling, selling, and selling made him one of our best salespeople.

Eventually, in a private meeting, I told him, "David, you are our best salesperson, but we have to let you go. I will help you get to your next job. I will help you with a month's pay and insurance. But it's time to go."

Of course, he was shocked and could not understand. He said, "Domenic, I am one of your best salespeople. How can you let me go?"

I agreed with his assessment. I told him, "You are one of the best I have seen. I am still letting you go because I do not believe we have the same values and goals."

Again, I want to clarify that David was not a bad person. He was not only an excellent salesperson but also a great guy.

He was a bad fit.

Let me add that not only would the team have to pick up his slack, but I would also have to do some of his work later. This extra work would not satisfy my Purpose in Life.

David went on to work with another company that fit his lone wolf, aggressive salesman value. A company that valued sales as much as he did and compensated him accordingly. A company that most likely did not need a team mentality—just a sell, sell, sell mentality.

When last we spoke, he was thriving.

A Value-Driven Team in Action

I loved visiting our clients with large estates. I loved the sounds, the colors, and the smells: fruit trees, bees, and that positive Mother Nature vibe. One beautiful spring day, I was walking the grounds of one of my favorite clients. She also loved walking the property, a working farm with orchids, veggie gardens, horse stables, and topiaries.

That day, she was home, so she joined me on my walk, decked out in her farmer's attire: the boots, the overalls, the hat, the works. She seemed to be part of the property. We admired everything as we walked, but I knew she was ready to create something new. Something that would make the property feel like the farm that it was.

However, for high-end clients, a farm is never a farm, and the value of "service the client, period" can have serious consequences.

These clients want what they want when they want it.

Since "I is an engineer," a la Dad's verbiage. I created an environment with systems and resources to make this happen. We were *always* ready to make this happen. The things we pulled off seemed like magic, but it was just preparation, preparation, and then some more preparation.

So there we were, walking the property together, admiring this and that, inhaling the sweet smells of spring trees and flowers. When we stopped by the topiary garden, my client commented, "These red tulips are getting a little past their prime. What do you think about planting Nico-blue pansies?"

I thought that was a great idea, so I asked, "What did you have in mind, and when would you like to do it?"

"How about this week? For the weekend?"

It was Monday, and this was no small space.

We had a team ready to make magic happen. We had growers stocked with plenty of flowers and deliverers to pick them up and deliver them. We had material companies for soil. Extra workers to move over from other projects. Workers to prep and plant. Waterers. Cleanup and debris removal teams and processes.

I ran the math.

It would take an estimated eighty-plus hours of prepping and planting, including moving workers and finding and delivering the flowers—two days without issues would get us done on Wednesday.

We agreed and set the work in motion.

We delivered the flowers in about eight thousand pots, and then eight workers spent the day installing them.

When I showed the client the flowers on Wednesday afternoon, she said, "Dom, these pansies seem a bit too purple. Can you find a more Nico-Blue blue?"

Most companies would have a nervous breakdown, but we had a value: "Service the Client, Period." Not just in words but in actions, too. I said, "No problem." We agreed to donate the others to a local church, and I went to find a more Nico-blue blue.

I had to assign more men to the task. Unfortunately, our regular grower didn't have the right flower color in the needed quantities. Not to worry—our office found them in the next state.

We finished planting the new Nico-blue flowers by late Thursday night.

As our client examined our new work, she was puzzled. "Dom, don't you think these are too powdery blue?"

You may think I was thinking evil, crazy thoughts: *These are Nico blue. F me, we did all this work!*

My reaction was genuine and much different: "Of course I do."

She pondered momentarily and asked, "What do you think of yellow pansies?"

Off we went again with the delivery and the hours and the work.

When we showed her the results, she stopped and said, "Wow, I really don't like yellow. Can you please find Nico Blue? I had my heart set on that color."

By now, it was Friday. She was hosting her friends for a tea brunch and needed the project completed for Sunday. I said, "Of course. I saw just the Nico blue you are looking for today!"

Before I go on, I want you to know I have worked with this client for eight years. I learned how she thought and knew what she loved. I don't want to make it sound like I hoodwinked her. We had a special bond, and if things played out like I thought they might, I stored the first set of pansies—all eight thousand pots—on the other side of her twenty-five-acre home.

After we replaced the yellow with the first batch, I (mentally) closed my eyes and held my breath as we walked to the garden again.

"Now that's what I call Nico blue! Beautiful, beautiful, beautiful. Thank you."

Her tea brunch went splendidly. The churches loved her powder-blue and yellow donations. We didn't charge her for the last delivery or material. Most importantly, no one complained about the three different plantings. The team was just as proud of their accomplishments as she was of her gorgeous Nico-blue garden.

I was proud of the team, who oozed our values as they "serviced the client, period."

Hire for the Future

Remember my roundtable mentoring session? A business owner asked me, "What do you think is the key to making people come to the table? How do we get them to do what we want?"

I replied, "I do not believe you can make anyone come to the table. You cannot make anyone do anything."

For an employee to become more and do more, they need to *want* to do more.

Hiring employees based on their values gives you the best chance of contributing. Having employees with the same values can be the first key to great employees. Remember, those values come from your Purpose in Life and become your culture.

You are doing something that not many business owners are willing to do. You have started doing something new for your life and company. Becoming a leader and leaving behind a command-and-control business is very uncomfortable.

Many owners stay in a command-and-control mindset, trying to do everything that needs to be done. They wear the many hats of sales, production, accounting, and anything else that will keep the wheels of the machine turning. If you believe that all you need to do is do more of the same thing—command more people and control more outcomes—I promise you will hit a wall.

You created and grew your company to this point, which is a great accomplishment. I know what it feels like. However, in my experience, what I did to achieve a certain level of growth did not get me where I wanted to go.

What you did to get where you are today will not get you to that future company. It will create more chaos and more issues. It will take away that valuable "gone, never to return" time from everything else in your life.

The change and the new way have already started. The old way will require you to spend more and more time trying to bring the Davids back in line. This behavior results in a revolving door of hiring and firing, which is not money-making time.

You are becoming a Tomato Paste Leader. The new way will take you to the Strategic Objective you aspire to reach. Armed with Company Values and an Organizational Chart with positions, you have the tools to hire for values. This first step in Employee Development is the change that will transform good potential employees into great employees.

You are at that point of growing, making more sales, having more clients, and now hiring more employees. If you also wonder why making more sales is not generating more profit with more work, it begins with you and your employees. It starts right in the hiring stage.

This process is for you, the company, *and* your employees. When leaders invest in their team to that extent right from the beginning, in the hiring stage, the team gives back much more.

You are building a future where every team member brings their best self to the table—where, together, you create something truly remarkable. Next, let's talk about how to keep those right-fit people at the table once they show up.

INGREDIENT 5:
Orientation

"Everyone talks about building a relationship with your customer. I think you build one with your employees first."

—Angela Ahrendts, Senior Vice President, Apple

One bright, sunny afternoon, my general contractor and brother Michael took me on a ride to some of his construction projects in New York City.

I watched his workers build scaffolding on a new building repair project. It was fascinating how they built the first sections and continued up the building. I could see how the scaffolding protected the people under the structure and gave the building extra strength before the workers started building and repairing it.

Once the building is complete, the support is removed, and it can stand independently.

In this next section of Employee Development, you want to accomplish the same for the new hire. You want to build a scaffold around the new employees, giving them extra strength and help as the team serves the client and the business.

Welcoming a new employee is an opportunity to shape their journey within your organization and ensure they can survive and thrive in the new environment. Providing structure and assistance during the early stages of employment is a critical first step in nurturing talent, fostering a sense of belonging, and equipping the new talent for a successful and fulfilling career in your company. It creates an environment where they have the opportunity and motivation to learn.

Building a support system around your employees helps them achieve more than they think is possible once they can finally stand independently.

To prepare your new hires for success, provide them with a mentor-guided learning orientation period. This allows your new employee to learn while having the support and expertise of a team member. Outstanding employees will quickly distinguish themselves during this phase. Value-driven employees will either align with an organization that reflects those values or show they are not a good fit.

Orientation will show the employees how the company highlights its commitment to investing in its employees' growth and development. This commitment can foster a sense of empowerment and loyalty throughout the entire company. It is a significant, loud signal to the employee that the organization prioritizes values alignment and will foster an environment where they can thrive.

Key Concepts

- **Positive First Impression:** An effective orientation program gives employees a positive first impression, allowing them to feel welcome, informed, and prepared. It is vital for ensuring an employee's long-term success within your organization.

- **Mentoring from the Start:** Mentoring starts in the beginning, with a thorough orientation program that explains the various aspects of company culture, values, policies, job roles, and system training. This sets the stage for ongoing mentorship and support throughout their tenure.

- **Clear Onboarding Plan:** An effective orientation program includes a clear onboarding plan with a schedule for learning, milestones to create forward movement, and resources to help new hires settle into their roles.

This clarity helps new employees navigate their initial days with confidence.

- **Team Integration:** Introducing new employees to their teams and departments fosters a collaborative, interconnected work environment. This helps new hires build relationships, understand team dynamics, and feel like valued members.

- **Evaluation and Feedback:** Building an evaluation process into the orientation plan helps the company assess the new employee's fit, values alignment, and potential path for career development. Regular feedback sessions provide opportunities for adjustment and growth.

CHAPTER 16 :
Learning Leadership from Cheesecake

"Someone's sitting in the shade today because someone planted a tree a long time ago."

—Warren Buffett

After a long afternoon of shopping our tails off at the mall, my wife and I took our daughters to the Cheesecake Factory for dinner. By "our tails," I mean my tail held the packages while their tails decided what to buy.

The two hostesses at the front desk were kind and cheerful and seemed eager to help when we asked for a table. They gave us a buzzer and told us it would be a fifteen-minute wait.

One of the hostesses escorted us to the table as soon as the buzzer vibrated. She gave us our menus and asked if everything seemed satisfactory before leaving.

Then, the parade began.

A waiter immediately came to our table and filled our five water glasses. Next, two waitresses came to our table. One of them explained a new trainee was shadowing her. They asked what drinks we wanted and if we had any questions about the menu. We ordered drinks and an appetizer. I noticed a glass wall separating the kitchen from the main area, where we could see all the chefs and helpers hustling and bustling.

Soon after, a different waiter came by with the drinks and another with the appetizer. Then, the waitress and her trainee returned to check on us and give us tips about the best items on the menu. They took our entree orders, and off they went.

The people and food kept flowing like clockwork throughout the meal.

My coaching and engineering sides started to kick in. This was a thing of beauty. How was everyone doing the things that they were supposed to do?

I was musing about what a great business model this was when the waitress and trainee returned to try to get us to order that delicious cheesecake they are so famous for.

From the corner of my eye, I could see my wife and daughters watching me with that "Oh *no*. What is dad going to say?" look in their eyes. They knew what was coming. (Remember Ben & Jerry's?)

I couldn't resist. I knew how the waitstaff would answer, but I like hearing it myself. I was like a moth to a flame.

"Excuse me," I asked the waitress and trainee. "I noticed that you are all so organized. How is it that you all know what you are doing?"

She told me about how intense hiring was—about a two-week process, not for the faint of heart—followed by continuing training programs monthly and then yearly. Even the person who washed the dishes had a week's training. Holy cow!

I told them what a great meal experience it was and how much I appreciated their work. Then I stopped the dad-babbling, as there was no need to further embarrass my wife and daughters.

When I returned home that night, I quickly googled "Cheesecake Factory." What I found was pleasantly surprising. The firm spent an annual average of $2,000 on training for each employee, covering 46,000 employees at over 300 locations. A

$92 million-a-year expense just for training. (I would call it an investment instead of an expense, but what do I know?)

The CEO was quoted in an article explaining his hiring process and finding the right fit (sound familiar?). Cheesecake Factory would only hire employees with the same values who were willing to learn and do the work the way the company wanted them to. He explained that having those expectations in the hiring and training took much more time and money. "Still," he added, "we retain our employees."

I had to print this article out and give it to my partner the next day since investing in hiring, orientation, and career development had been one of many thorns and differences between our leadership styles.

I knew that training needed to start the moment we hired someone. However, it had been an uphill battle for me to take the time to train our new hires in the company's positions, systems, and values while still completing our work on time and growing our company.

My partner was less enthusiastic than I was about this part of our growth.

"We're going to spend all this time and money on them. What if they leave?"

"Teaching takes time out of their day when they could be making us money."

"We are wasting valuable resources and losing profits—profits for us!"

The Cheesecake Factory article made me feel I was on the right track. After all, they happily enjoyed sales of $1,000 per square foot—twice the national average for their industry—and one of the highest employee retention rates.

This was a pivotal period in our journey. Looking back on the company's growth, our sales rocketed from $2.5 million to $5 million. I know this orientation step of our Employee Development Program was part of this growth. This stellar growth happened within a year and a half. We no longer had to do everything ourselves. We truly were working smarter—*all* of us were.

(If you're still wondering, we chose the Toasted Marshmallow S'mores Galore for dessert.)

This time-consuming orientation task will be how you continue your journey as a growing leader. When an employee starts in a position, your orientation task creates solid scaffolding. The scaffolding is an environment in which the person hired with the owner's values is given the know-how and support to do the work the owner wants so they can do the job just like the owner would.

Employees put their trust in you, and they invest in you and the company. What return are you giving them on that investment?

These questions and ideas may seem counterintuitive to you as an owner. You invest much of your time, energy, and life into the business. Isn't a paycheck enough? As my partner would say, "I am paying them to do what I need them to do."

We are starting to mentor and grow employees without commanding or controlling them.

"Always" is a powerful word, yet I *always* see a shift when a client in my coaching practice starts to make that transformation. A shift happens when a leader transforms from working as this glorified worker-owner to leading with mentoring visionary leadership. When a leader is willing to invest time and money in their people, the next thing happens: an employee transformation. But this happens *only* when the leader makes this shift.

Consider what might happen if you invested your time, energy, and business life into your employees like you do the company.

I will show you how to make your investment worth it. We will delve into the mechanics of a successful orientation program that gives your team members the tools they need to thrive and make a difference from the beginning of their journey with you. We'll explore the components of a transformative orientation process and why each part matters.

I will show you how to build a scaffold to create a comprehensive picture of an ideal onboarding process.

All that's left to consider is whether you are ready to do the work necessary to make the extraordinary happen.

CHAPTER 17:
Level Up Your Orientation Process

"You can't stay in your corner of the forest waiting for others to come to you. You have to go to them sometimes."

—A. A. Milne, *Winnie the Pooh*

New employees aren't just workers; they are now part of your company's fabric. Orientation is an invitation for them to feel at home.

Orientation is the compass that guides new employees through the labyrinth of your organization's systems and culture. It sets the stage for their success and integration, allowing them to contribute effectively to your team.

Building a company where trust, connection, and participation are the norms, not the exceptions, requires a collective effort. You can't accomplish this alone. You also can't establish it in a one-time event. The initial weeks of a new hire's job set the tone for your working relationship. A comprehensive orientation process starts this relationship on the right footing, creating a solid foundation for ongoing learning and development.

The time, energy, and money you invest in each other starts on their first day.

The First Meeting

Orientation commences on the employee's first day and extends for three months. The first meeting sets the cornerstone for the mentorship to come, and ongoing weekly meetings become the foundation of the orientation process. Taking a holistic approach to orientation, in which the new employee is guided by a mentor, fosters team members' trust, connection, and participation from day one.

Mentors come in all sizes and shapes. I was the initial mentor for my employees, and I needed to be to ensure this employee development pilot program worked. In your organization, a mentor may be a department manager, an owner, or a coworker.

The point is to give a new employee someone to lean on and learn from.

In each meeting, the mentor comes prepared with specific tools, packets, and objectives. For example, in the first meeting, the mentor will be armed with an HR Employee Packet, the employee's personal Operations Manual, the Employee Handbook, and an education/mentoring program.

To ensure a smooth onboarding process, the mentor provides an easy-to-follow summary on the front cover of the packet. Each summary item has its corresponding section and a check-off space when completed.

The HR employee packet is the administrative component of the onboarding process. It contains the forms and information the company requires from the new employee to meet all federal, state, and company requirements. The packet is created in HR and returned to the new employee once signed. (This is the first time the new employee will see the connective tissues of departments and the teamwork between the two departments.)

An employee handbook references specific company policies, holidays, sick time, attire, etc.

An Operations Manual introduces the new employee to the company, its values and culture, expected results, specific details of their position, the various systems that run the company, and any templates and tools they'll have to fulfill their responsibilities.

You may already have an Organizational Bible—a complete guide for living, playing, and working in the company—or you may wonder how to build one. In an upcoming chapter, we will discuss this further when we integrate systems and delegation.

For now, focus on implementing these foundational tools (Organizational Chart, Position Agreement, and orientation plan) to set the stage for a successful onboarding journey.

These three tools will level you up in ways few other companies can pull off.

This process exemplifies what a sound system can do for employees. I am always excited about even the simplest system. These templates and programs, available at TomatoPasteLeadership.com/bonus, are a little taste of what is in store for you as we work toward systems.

You, the mentor, don't have to think about what to do with the new employee. You follow the step-by-step summary page and fill out the form corresponding to the summary item. A sound system lets you spend less time thinking about what steps you are taking and more time focusing on what is important: the new employee and how they work, act, and feel.

At ninety days, health insurance, profit-sharing, 401(k), education programs, and many federal and state laws kick in, meaning you'll make an even more significant financial investment. Before that transition, I wanted to know if the employee was the right fit for the role. If what they said during the hiring stage differed from who they said they were or the values were not there, I needed to let them go before I invested any further in them. Remember, if a recruit must move on from the company, you are not letting them go because they are a "bad" person but a "not a good fit" person.

Hold onto your shorts; now's the time to discuss planning your orientation program.

Orientation as a Mentoring Program

Career development can and should extend beyond the orientation period, but the expectations are set in these first three months. When orientation is considered a mentoring program, it creates a structured and comprehensive onboarding experience. It allows new employees to acclimate to your organization's culture, become proficient in their roles, and begin their journey toward leadership.

The program can be tailored to your organization and industry, but here is an example of an outline:

- Month 1: Building Foundations

    o   Week 1: Welcome and Introductions

    o   Week 2–3: Company Culture and Values

    o   Week 4–5: Systems Training

- Month 2: Integration and Skill Development

    o   Week 6–7: Role-Specific Training

    o   Week 8–9: Team Collaboration

    o   Week 10–11: Communication and Client Interaction

- Month 3: Leadership and Ongoing Development

    o   Week 12: Review and Feedback

    o   Week 13: Leadership Training

    o   Week 14–15: Final Evaluation

If some of these topics seem familiar, we've already covered quite a few. The work you did to name your values, create positions, and visualize the whole organization in a chart that flows from one department to another allowed you to establish culture and values, train to roles, and facilitate collaboration and communication. The rest—systems, reviews and feedback, and leadership—will be covered in the remainder of this book.

Map each process step so that each mentoring session follows a clear plan and produces results for you and the employee. Be sure to include training on any systems they will use, who they'll be working with, dates and times for benchmarks, and any resources that might help them succeed.

Start Well: The Facility Tour

Introductions to the department and each part of the company help a new employee start their collaboration with the team on the right foot. They also let the company know who this new person is and their position. This small but essential part of orientation has been missing in many companies I have visited or coached.

Incorporating a well-organized facility tour and employee introduction sets the tone for a workplace where employees feel valued, supported, and integrated into the team from day one. Creating an environment where everyone is introduced and welcomed fosters community and collaboration, ultimately contributing to a more positive and successful work experience.

End Well: The Evaluation Process

At the heart of an effective orientation process is determining whether the individual fits your company, ensuring the best possible alignment between their skills, values, and position.

During these initial three months of employment, you can closely observe the new employee in each mentorship meeting and their progressive interactions with the team as they settle into their role. This process also presents a chance to initiate a career development plan (we'll explore this concept in the next chapter) and align their strengths to a role where they can thrive.

Suppose the employee possesses the organization's values but needs a more suitable role. In that case, consider offering them a different position. Suppose it becomes evident that an employee doesn't align with the company's values. In that case, addressing this misalignment is essential, which might ultimately involve helping them transition to a different company that better fits their values.

By offering the proper support, acknowledging a misalignment when it arises, and working together to find suitable solutions, you set the stage for a thriving workforce and a harmonious environment, whether or not that specific employee remains part of it.

A Successful Orientation Should Include:

- **An Employee Packet:** This package contains all the information and forms necessary for the company and the employee. It showcases your commitment to collaboration.

- **The Employee's Personal Operations Manual:** This document guides living, playing, and working within the company. It offers a detailed understanding of the company's culture and values, the employee's role, and the systems in place.

- **Information about Your Education/Mentoring Program:** A well-defined plan for the three-month orientation, including training, system familiarization, meeting schedules, and available resources.

- **A Tour of the Facility/Employee Introductions:** These are small but essential gestures that help the new employee integrate into the team and enable the organization to meet its latest members.

- **An Overview of the Evaluation Process:** A three-month review allows you to assess whether the employee fits the company. If values align but the role isn't ideal, consider offering a different position.

The Way Forward (for Everyone on the Team)

This process is not about passing judgment or putting your new hire through a series of trials but ensuring that the employee and the company are on the same path to success. Executing effectively creates an opportunity to nurture growth, alignment, and development. It also builds a dynamic and value-driven organization where employees can find *their* best fit.

The next ingredient will cover career development plans in more detail, where you will provide employees with the tools and resources they need to excel within your organization.

The easy part is creating these maps, packets, and plans. The not-so-easy part is implementing them, especially when you need to reorient your existing employees to this new value-driven way of being.

It's often said you can't teach an old dog new tricks. Adapting to change is a crucial skill in the ever-evolving business landscape.

However, this was not on my mind when I set this orientation program in motion and individually guided my existing employees through it. I foolheartedly believed that our existing people would be thrilled to become part of this new transformation, and I also expected our people to be able to adapt.

In our journey as entrepreneurs, my partner and I faced the daunting task of keeping pace with changing dynamics as our company grew and our positions and values became more significant. Meaning we *were* the old dogs trying to learn new tricks.

I found this orientation process difficult initially because it was new to me. I needed more leadership skills but was willing to learn and take that messy path toward transformation. Remember, I had those beautiful daughters nudging me along (to put it mildly).

My business partner found this transformation extremely challenging. Surprisingly, the old guard employees also found it difficult.

I was doing my best to give them the same opportunity to survive and grow as I would give the new employees. So, I offered the old guard the same twelve weeks of mentorship and guidance in their new position as I would give the value-driven new hires.

The one-result positions of the Organizational Chart didn't work for them—and frighteningly, the whole process didn't work for most of them.

A chasm formed between our many-hat, micromanaged employees and the fresh, value-driven talent we had begun to hire. This chasm was one of the main reasons I was the primary mentor.

On one hand, our newly hired employees, each assigned a single position, were thriving. They were working toward their specific results and responsibilities as a team. They welcomed my mentorship (initially, I was the company's only mentor) and were willing to learn.

You could see that these employees, who had been guided through an orientation process from the beginning, were well on their way to more substantial success and a better chance of survival with the company.

On the other hand, our seasoned employees, who were used to doing whatever it took to get the job done, struggled to adapt to the changing landscape.

Throughout my journey, I've learned that progress is often a dance of two steps forward and one step back. However, this transition felt like one step forward and three steps back. What puzzled me was that these two groups found themselves at odds—there was so much resistance to the idea of holding one position.

One key lesson that became apparent was that every company possesses values and culture, whether explicitly defined or embraced. Our organization was no exception. My partner and I had taken on every task around us, so it was no surprise that our employees mirrored this pattern. They did everything they were asked (or commanded) to do, much to the detriment of our organization's stability.

I won't sugarcoat it—this period of growth and transformation was undeniably messy. The most bittersweet part was the realization that we would inevitably lose some of our long-standing employees. Employees who had been with the organization for a substantial amount of time and worked hard struggled to transition into team players. I was torn between our loyalty to these individuals and the need to operate in a new way.

The one bright spot was seeing the foundation we laid in our hiring and orientation process so clearly. We had emphasized alignment with company values, which was paying off in our new employees. Looking back, the transformation could have been more seamless had we established this foundation earlier.

This is why I heavily stress the first section of this book in my coaching practice. I know how difficult it is for owners to establish a foundation first (Purpose in Life, Strategic Objective, Company Values, and Organizational Charts). I had that "been there, done that" mindset, too—who needs the foo-foo BS of a foundation when you have to build, build, build systems, systems, systems? I know that none of those processes work without laying the foundation first.

Every step of this transformation was undoubtedly worth it. My story, my journey, and the inevitable craziness of the transition period were accompanied by fantastic growth and personal and organizational transformation.

Embrace the complexities of organizational change. Through these struggles, companies genuinely transform, taking everyone in the organization from wherever you are now to the kind of success you've only dreamed of.

CHAPTER 18:
No Yelling Required

"One day, if you have a little bit of talent and a lot of hard work, you're going to find out who you are."

—Massimo Bottura

When a leader mentors an employee, teaches education skills or guides soft skills, a culture of learning begins to form. In a thriving environment, leaders foster this culture, allowing all employees to grow intellectually, emotionally, and financially.

I was lucky to have coaches, especially my dad. Thanks to these stellar coaches, I went from being a hardworking business owner to the leader and mentor of four multimillion-dollar businesses and a coach for companies that excelled even more.

Don't let me tell you that transformation is all peaches and cream. I must admit, I still remember how I had to be dragged, kicking, scratching, and screaming as I was becoming a leader and mentor.

In a time long ago and a galaxy far, far away—back when I used the Italian "loud and passionate" method of management and leadership—I recall talking on the phone with a foreman. A crowd of employees were working around me. Not knowing my ass from my elbow, I wanted to impress everyone in the room with my leadership panache. I believed this included screaming my thoughts and decisions.

I also used to "mentor" at high volume. I could blame it on my Italian way of explaining things loudly, but that would be an excuse.

Fortunately, I had a secret weapon in my executive coach. He came to our facility weekly to meet with my employees and me, and once every month, he and I had a solid day strategizing in his Rhode Island office.

We worked on leadership mentoring, life and business strategies, and project management there, and then I drove the two hours back home with mashed potatoes for brains.

Our once-a-month session usually went like this: We discussed what I did last month, including what worked and what didn't. We then discussed how I handled situations with employees, my partner, and my family since he knew my Purpose in Life. He received project updates, system development notes, etc. In addition to helping me through this profound transition in life and business, his sessions taught me to do the same kind of mentoring with my employees.

I told him how I handled a call during one of our executive coaching sessions. I proudly described it as "loud and demonstrative." I explained, "I wanted to show the employees and interns how an owner and leader acts."

He waited for me to finish, looked me in the eye, and said, "Who the hell do you think you are, yelling like that? You didn't act like a leader. You acted like an asshole."

I needed to hear that. Most of us believe that employees will understand if we show our passion by yelling and screaming.

When I returned to the office that day, I apologized to the employee for that phone conversation and to the group that had been there, listening to my "leadership" demonstration.

I think back on that mentoring session with one hell of a smile—I remember commenting to him that I was paying him a lot of money to call me an asshole.

After an exhausting week with my executive coach, I was given an opportunity to showcase my journey as a better leader.

One late Sunday evening, I was relaxing with my family, watching the Disney movie *Mulan*, when I got a frantic call from my partner.

He shouted, "I just sat down to do some work and can't do my invoicing! Half of the backup is missing from every client's packet. Now, I cannot do anything. I know you hired a new person. Who is this person? Why did you hire her? I told you she was a mistake. Do something!"

I thought, *Sunday at 8:00 p.m.? Invoicing? Do something? What on earth can I do at this hour?"*

I told him I would not start calling employees, especially not my new hire. I told him to try to do as much as he could with the paperwork that he had. Yes, I would help him—in the morning.

He continued until it became clear that he could not get me to do what he wanted, at which point he abruptly hung up the phone.

The new hire my partner was so upset about was about two months into her orientation. Her name was Lucy. My partner and I were 180-degree opposites when hiring her.

My partner wanted a more corporate-type person—someone with a master's degree, someone who would dress in a suit, someone of a higher educational caliber.

Don't get me wrong. I believe in higher education and experiential self-education. I was always looking for values that would make a great fit. In this instance, I was glad to be the operations manager, with the final say over all departmental hires and fires.

I was amazed at how much she exuded the company's values, was teachable, and wanted to be part of a great team.

I remember her telling me she loved using systems because she used them in her previous job. She gave examples of working with teams, talked about the books she read, and mentioned the two business courses she'd taken at the community college. She didn't know everything about her role yet but was willing to learn. Even how she organized her paperwork during the interview screamed "good fit."

Her position was information management, and she was responsible for controlling all information that entered and left the organization and managing client paperwork. Her tasks involved managing the company's phones, emails, and mail, as well as all file management and management of client profiles. This was one of the paperwork-flow stopgaps that connected production to accounting.

One of the most critical tasks in her position was that she was the first person a client or anyone spoke to when they contacted the company. It sounds simple, but I highly value this task.

I was also Lucy's mentor.

I arrived at work on Monday morning at about 9:00 a.m. Yes, nine. The production department started at six, but remember; I had systems running the business and great people to run the systems. I preferred to have breakfast with my girls instead of hovering over everyone in the office for the first hours of the day.

My right-hand man in production, Julio, was a fantastic manager, mentor, and delegator. If Julio or the production department needed me before nine, they would call me, but even that was rare. If mistakes happened while I wasn't there, they were learning opportunities. (I can think of plenty of learning opportunities I had in that position.)

It had taken a lot of work, strategically and tactically, to get to that point, but everything was working marvelously. Before I stepped into my office, over twenty-five crews were scheduled, readied, and sent into the field each morning.

This morning was different. As soon as I walked in, my right hand—the liaison position—and, incidentally, Lucy's sister—

was looking out the window door, distressed, waiting to meet me.

"Dom, you have to do something; my sister, Lucy, is about to leave. She is quitting."

I rushed to the office and found my new employee in tears.

My partner arrived at work before me and reprimanded her immediately. Of course, he wanted to know what had happened, but he also wanted to vent his frustration.

As you might have noticed, my partner was not the mentoring type. He was a salesman—one of the best—but a mentor? A teacher? No. He was an old-dog-no-new-tricks kind of guy.

He "mentored" with much yelling and venting, an "I'm the boss; hear me roar" mentality.

Now that I knew better, I sat my new protégé down and tried to calm her shaking nerves.

My first step was to listen to her and understand what had happened.

She told me the wall of filing cabinets was full, so she attempted to clean it. This meant archiving part of that client's file.

I was impressed with her initiative and told her so. Although she had just started in this position, this was a great way to see her problem-solving values already in action.

I was proud of her.

After I calmed the situation down, I talked to my partner about it and demanded that he apologize to her. After much prodding, he did.

You may say, "Hey, Domenic, you need to solve the real problem: your new employee and the breakdown."

Lucy was a bright, fresh, out-of-the-box protégé with so much potential. I needed her to give us one more chance. After I told her I was proud of her, I said, "Lucy, I apologize for my partner's outburst. If you can give me a chance to explain, I want you to continue working with us."

She agreed—at least to keep listening.

The issue was a simple misunderstanding about the client profile system, and the solution was education. I explained how the client profile management system worked for the company, how she worked with it in her department, and how the department that followed hers used the profiles for invoicing.

It was like a light bulb went off in her head. I was proud of Lucy for taking the initiative. Yet, she saw how her work affected the other departments and quickly understood what she'd done to upset the system's flow.

No yelling was required.

She apologized for her mistake. I told her that this was how orientation was meant to work and that mistakes were to be expected.

One of the best ways to teach and mentor is through mistakes. I loved it when issues like these arose because they allowed me to teach. And how we respond when things don't go as planned becomes an opportunity to demonstrate our values.

I added that she should continue challenging our systems and looking for improvement. Because we were in the mentoring period and she was unfamiliar with the flows, she should talk to her mentor before making serious system moves. But I didn't want her to stop.

Empowering new hires with mentor-led orientation can elevate your employees' success and align your business with its core values. With each orientation phase, you are sowing the seeds of a stronger, more cohesive team and a prosperous future.

The journey doesn't end here; it's only just begun.

That afternoon, she immediately put the client profiles back together, and all was well in the world.

She became a tremendous asset for years to come to her team and the company.

I can still hear her voice as she answered every phone call with the values of "Service the Client, Period, and "Image."

"Good morning. This is BEST Business and Life Strategies. My name is Lucy. How can I help you?"

As you conclude this chapter, remember that your leadership journey is not just about acclimating new hires to their roles; it's also about setting the stage for their ongoing growth and development.

I can't forget Lucy and how she tasted two types of mentoring. I can't help but smile at my own experience with paying my executive coach to call me an asshole.

Yet effective mentorship can be the difference between stagnation and success.

As you continue your voyage of discovery, keep your values and your company's Strategic Objective at the forefront. Let these documents guide you toward a future where your team thrives, and your business reaches unprecedented heights.

This is just the beginning.

In the next ingredient, we'll delve deeper into employee development, providing employees with the tools and resources they need to grow and prosper within your organization and find their potential throughout their careers.

You read that right. As the leader and owner, you provide something very different from the typical organization.

INGREDIENT 6:
Career Development

"This is the secret to success. If you want to succeed in work, love, friendship, and life, give the people around you a great return on whatever it is they invest in you."

—Donald Miller, *Business Made Simple*

This essence of career development is an often overlooked yet vital aspect of an organization's success. Donald says it is a secret, and I can confirm that it escapes many business owners.

I was one of these owners.

For years, my vision of our company being on the verge of becoming something bigger and better didn't resonate as I had anticipated. In the pre-transformation era, the mere mention of growth didn't stir up excitement; it stirred up hostility among our seasoned employees.

Eyes rolled, and dissent echoed through the office.

"How do you expect us to do more work?"

"We are already overwhelmed and working at maximum capacity."

"WTF, Domenic?"

Despite the resistance, the company kept growing, but that growth was accompanied by perpetual upheaval. They were skeptical of what I was doing.

I wanted my employees to embrace this new Strategic Objective, the values, and their new positions.

I was determined to set things right, so I delved deeper into what I felt was the right path. I built new and more powerful systems, doubled down on hiring for values, and conducted time-intensive orientations.

Then I uncovered something. The pivotal shift I was looking for would only occur when I recognized the relationship between the employees' growth and our organizational success. Employees could align their professional growth with the company's vision—and I could help them!

That was when I established what we will discuss in this chapter: individual mentorship programs. I was no longer a job provider; I was a career developer. The Julios, Minas, and others could thrive in an organization that didn't just promise growth but supported it with actual actions.

This commitment, this transformation, wasn't just for the betterment of the organization; it was a holistic, transformative experience for everyone involved. My commitment to my employees extended beyond their employment. It was a promise to help our people reach their aspirations and life goals.

Synergy began to develop between me, a growing leader, and our team, the value-driven employees. Our dynamic shifted from "WTF, Domenic?" to "Wow, I am part of something bigger, Domenic."

What was once skepticism transformed into a collective sense of purpose. This was mind-blowing for me.

It was the soul of our organization's transformation and embodied my value of creating an environment where everyone thrives professionally and financially.

Key Concepts

- **Mutually Beneficial Growth:** Your company's success hinges on the dedication and passion of your employees. In return, investing in their growth fosters a mutually beneficial relationship where both parties thrive.

- **Value of Exceptional Employees:** Exceptional employees are invaluable assets to your organization, driving profitability, efficiency, and client satisfaction. Investing in their development yields significant returns for your business.

- **Empowering Decision-Making:** Empowering employees to make owner-like decisions will foster autonomy and growth. Instead of allowing them to become task performers, focus on nurturing future leaders.

- **Demystifying Career Development:** Dispel the myth that significant investments in career development are reserved for elite organizations. Understand that developing your people isn't a post-success initiative; it's the engine that propels you toward success.

CHAPTER 19:
Reframe the Review

"You can have everything in life you want, if you will just help enough other people get what they want."

—Zig Ziglar

In the first decade of running our company, I sat down with each of my team members every year for a weird, forced, uncomfortable conversation. No matter how painful and unproductive it was, we'd meet the following year to do it all over again.

It was a necessary evil, endorsed by all the pooh-bahs at all the business conferences. It was what "great" companies did, or so I thought.

The annual performance review, that awkward ritual of dissecting past performances, rarely yielded positive outcomes. It had become a dreaded affair for us all. I felt trapped in it.

The primary objective was clear: dole out perks such as pay raises, performance bonuses, and extra vacation time. The price for these rewards was an annual beatdown session, thinly tolerated awkwardness, and the illusion of accountability.

I always harbored doubts about the effectiveness of those meetings.

So, as the winds of change swept through my company, the performance review was one of the first things to vanish into thin air.

We didn't stop meeting but rebranded them to match our new hiring approach, where values took precedence over skills. Since one of those values was creating an environment to thrive, performance reviews were reshaped into "career development sessions."

A performance review measures skills, but a career development session is a way to check in with employees to see if they are thriving, growing, learning, and advancing.

Recentering Our Focus

What does it mean to be employee-centric?

Owners often tout their dedication to their teams' well-being, but actions speak louder than words. Most educational programs fall short, and employee development happens sporadically. A cloud of mistrust looms between owners and employees.

There's also a reluctance to invest, a fear that spending time and resources on employees might not yield a tangible return, or worse, they will leave anyway.

I used to get this from one of my partners when we were growing. I can hear him now:

"Why the hell should we spend time, resources, and money on them when they are just going to leave?"

"They work; we pay them."

"We need them working. That's how we make money."

"Stop wasting time. Time is money."

My partner and the many owners I coached through this concern have solid points. If an employee is only there for a paycheck and will leave when better money comes, why should you invest time and resources in developing them?

Investing significantly in career development does come with uncertainty. Because of this, many think companies must reach a specific sales or profit level to justify the expense.

I have encountered countless well-meaning organizations that claim to prioritize employees and their needs. Yet, they fail to align their actions with an actual commitment to employee growth. This is where the trust erodes.

We reached that top 3 percent *because* of our investment in people.

A fundamental shift in perspective accelerated my evolution toward something more than a worker-owner.

My employees didn't work for me; I worked for them.

Holy shit, did I say that?

I'm not alone, though.

I came across an article that included a survey done by PricewaterhouseCoopers, the world's second-largest professional services network. They posed this question to over 40,000 employees:

"What do employees seek and value most in their positions or roles?"

Their answers may surprise you. They did me.

1. Growth

2. Development

3. Money

While money is undeniably crucial, it didn't top the list. People were seeking growth and development *before* financial rewards.

This shouldn't be surprising, but it is. Looking back at where we started, how we navigated each step, and when we finally landed among the industry's top tier, I can see that I craved something more than profit. The same can be said for my employees. They yearned for something beyond a paycheck, too.

Now, there's nothing inherently wrong with being part of the 87 percent of companies under $1 million in sales or the 10 percent between $1 million and $9 million. You don't have to wait until you reach the pinnacle to treat your employees well.

Providing employees with the tools they need to excel benefits them *and* translates into increased profits, more free time, and organic growth for the organization.

Armed with this knowledge, my team's goals and aspirations became as essential as the Purpose in Life and Strategic Objectives were for me.

My role transformed into a strategic, result-oriented position, just like I had created for the rest of the team. My responsibilities were to:

1. Craft a future vision and devise strategies to make it a reality.

2. Become a teacher of systems and a mentor of values.

3. Guide my employees in realizing their aspirations.

Our career development sessions helped me understand *their* visions and aspirations. I focused on leadership development, systems and flows, position support, technical and communication skills, projects, and computer literacy. With deeper insights into their goals, I could actively contribute to their development throughout the year, creating pathways for them to realize *their life purposes*.

It was more than just a meeting. It was a deeply held commitment. It made me more of the leader I envisioned. I could be a quiet leader who guided people toward their dreams. The organization and employees thrived together in this symbiotic relationship of mutual growth and support.

The gap between claiming employee-centricity and embodying it is wide. It's not merely about words; it's about a systematic, genuine commitment to employee growth. A paradigm shift will likely be needed. The key revelation is this: don't postpone your people's development until you hit certain sales thresholds or minimize it in annual reviews. Your people's development is what will propel you toward those milestones.

CHAPTER 20:
The Development Difference

"Train people well enough so they can leave. Treat them well enough so they don't want to."

—Richard Branson

Eagerly anticipated career development sessions were a game changer. Instead of an annual dread, they were the pulse of connection, growth, and shared aspirations within the team.

Ah, the exhilarating paradox of ownership: the task that used to send shivers down my spine became my passion.

Formally, I implemented them two times a year. I also checked in with each employee informally throughout the year. I relished collaborating with the exceptional individuals who invested so much time and energy in our organization. My employees, like us owners, weren't confined solely to the walls of our organization. They harbored dreams beyond our day-to-day, and I enjoyed understanding those dreams and playing a role in making them a reality.

I also knew that team intelligence was more competent than just Domenic intelligence.

The collective intelligence of the team surpasses the insights of any individual. Harnessing that intelligence as a resource is not just strategic; it's a testament to the wisdom of empowering those around you.

Someone who is a great fit and has excellent skills deserves continual development throughout their journey with the organization, however long that might be. It's not merely an investment in their role but a recognition of their potential to earn the keys to the castle: the ability to make owner-like decisions instead of waiting for an owner's commands.

Here's a radical proposition. Why persist with something universally disliked that yields marginal results when you could embark on something new, something transformative? Would you rather keep doing something that doesn't work and everybody hates or try something new that may change everything?

Choosing between the familiar and the inspirational could redefine your organization and the essence of how you lead and inspire.

Ready to take the leap?

If you're struggling to picture investing in your people this much, humor me for a moment.

How efficient are your annual reviews?

Do they help you get the most (or any more at all) out of anyone?

Have you ever sat on the other side of that table with all that discomfort and judgment coming at you?

How did that go?

This adage sums it up best: "Insanity is doing the same thing over and over again and expecting different results."

Career Development in Action

It was a stunning, sun-kissed morning when I sat down with Della, the dynamo spearheading the vendor management role in the accounts payable department. Through the doorway, I caught a glimpse of her gearing up for our career development session. She had a sparkle in her eyes, an unmistakable excitement that caught me off guard.

Although the term "performance reviews" had faded from our company vocabulary, remnants of the old mindset lingered for some.

A few employees hated those sessions no matter what I called them and relied instead on the mentality of "I work hard. Doesn't that count for everything?" I won't belittle anyone here, but there was more to my organization than just working hard and forgetting everything else—the values of systems, learning, growing, and each position's responsibilities.

Della was different, and her enthusiasm was contagious.

Back in the cozy confines of my office, Della, brimming with notes and ideas, was ready for a personal and professional conversation about her life.

The Flow of Conversation

I followed a systematic series of steps to structure our discussions, aligning with my belief that everything benefits from a system—even our career development sessions.

Here's a snapshot of how it went:

Before the meeting, I printed out the necessary forms and reports:

- Position Agreement

- Self-Evaluation Summary Form

- Compensation Report

- Employee Earning Summary Report for the year

Both the mentor and employee prepared for the meeting:

- Mentor:

  o Utilized the Compensation Report and the Employee Earning and Information Report.

  o Reviewed the previous Evaluation Report. Understand the goals and projects the employee worked on in the previous period.

  o Filled out the Compensation Report.

- Employee:

  o Reviewed their Position Agreement.

  o Completed the Self-Evaluation Summary Form and returned it.

  o Scheduled a career development meeting.

Then, in the career development meeting, the mentor and employee reviewed:

- How did the employee perform in their written Position Agreement?

- What projects were completed, and what were their statuses?

- Whether the employee's written goals were accomplished and the status of results.

- Whether the employee's education goals were accomplished and the status of results.

- Whether a raise was appropriate.

- Most importantly, how the employee would develop for the next period.

Around the intricate dance of reports and evaluations, the focus is on constructive feedback and collaborative goal-setting.

Della was ready.

She brought her Position Agreement. Her self-assessment. Her projects. Her future ideas and plans.

We went through the meeting process step by step. We looked at Della's position and results statement. We examined how she accomplished her position's results over the last six months—the good, the bad, the ugly—updating anything or noting anything that could improve those results. We looked at the strategy side of her position and the tasks. We reviewed her self-assessment. We reviewed her projects for the year. We looked at what worked and what didn't work.

Della's level of preparation was impressive, but what truly stood out were her one- and three-year career aspirations. In her assessment, she revealed a desire to delve into the financial aspects of our work—a revelation that left me in awe. Not just because she wanted to grow in her position but also because she acknowledged a gap in her knowledge and skill set that she wanted to close.

It is difficult for anyone to say, "I do not know enough about this subject," especially when it's the subject they were hired into. However, she was comfortable enough with me to let me know she was lacking in an area of her professional life.

For me, this was the purpose of our entire process. It was what Della had been so excited about and what I loved to do in every career development session. She knew she needed help getting there. I knew that if I helped her with her plan, she'd become a person to be reckoned with, and that would free me up to focus more on my role.

Della's aspirations led to a radical decision: a two- to three-year plan to enhance her financial skills. Since our benefits package included education, I recommended that she scout community colleges and take online courses. The incentive was simple: her commitment would determine the extent of financial support.

To no one's surprise, Della embraced the challenge, and the benefits to our company were immeasurable. She emerged from those classes financially adept, contributing significantly to her dreams and aspirations and our bottom line.

This wasn't micromanagement. It was mentorship. Della wanted to grow and be inspired. She knew the results would speak for themselves, so she took the owner-like initiative to make it happen.

In the grand tapestry of our company's growth, Della's story became a vibrant thread, weaving together individual employee aspirations and success with collective organizational success.

Career development is the pulse of success in your journey and the businesses you run. It isn't just one key—it's the master key that unlocks individual growth and drives the entire organization into new dimensions of success.

Della knew it. PricewaterhouseCoopers knew it. Zig knew it. And I saw it unfold. Career development isn't just a process; it's the heartbeat of a thriving, evolving organization.

Transforming Dreams into Realities

When I shared the future vision with the value-driven individuals I brought into our organization, there was a deep sense of empowerment and a shared understanding that we were accomplishing something extraordinary.

When leaders and employees merged into a team supporting each other, the worries of having more work to do no longer instilled fear; instead, there was a collective assurance that our organization had a future, and stagnation wasn't part of it.

For the few who did leave to pursue greener pastures, I wasn't upset that I had invested in them. I *still* take pride in being a part of their journey of professional growth, even though it led them to new horizons. So what if they "took advantage" of the investments I made in them? That was the plan all along. I yearned for employees with solid values to seize every opportunity to craft the lives of their dreams for themselves, their families, and the people they served.

Many more remarkable individuals like Della stayed. She excelled in her role and, in turn, granted me the freedom to cherish moments with my family, delve into strategic pursuits, and revel in what I loved: my family, employees, business, and community.

My vacations weren't just an escape; they were a joyous return, a chance to witness how each team member flourished in my absence. It was a time of shared learning—what worked, what didn't, how they navigated challenges, and their plans for the future. It allowed them to flex those owner-like muscles, and I encouraged that.

I relinquished control because I had developed into a leader. I had faith in the people and systems that shaped our company. Fueled by a collective spirit, we all reveled in the prospect of conquering the world as a team.

The formula for growing a business isn't simplistic; it's where theory meets reality and heroes emerge.

It was my privilege to nurture my employees into the heroes they aspired to become. By developing them, I discovered the true essence of leadership: the power to transform dreams into realities.

STEP 2:
Conclusion

"The growth and development of people is the highest calling of leadership."

—Harvey S. Firestone

My cousins Marcucio and Marietta hosted the kind of dinner you would expect in an Italian family's home on a Sunday evening: family, friends, children, great food, and lively conversations.

The dinner started with just a few people and one tray of pasta and meatballs.

Then, more families stopped by and sat down. Marietta loves this. She put out more settings with another tray of delicious pasta. The table grew with people and more trays. Out came more pasta, meatballs, chicken cutlets, eggplant, and trays of meats and cheeses. (Hey, you knew pasta and meatballs were just the starters.)

Everyone came with hungry stomachs and smiles on their faces.

This is what an Italian Sunday dinner is for any laypeople who might be reading (since there are two types of people in the world: Italians and non-Italians): lots of families and friends and delicious food.

Of course, eating without discussing life and the pursuit of happiness is not in our blood.

These Sunday discussions can become very lively. This one—a discussion after COVID-19—was no exception.

We all agreed on the problems COVID-19 had caused for grade-level students. The youngest of our family lost so much in those two years of education. We agreed that remote and hybrid learning was not conducive to good education at that level. Both the teachers and the students were exasperated.

Sadly, most schools and universities needed more time to prepare to teach using a remote method. We weren't blaming them, but it seemed ironic that our schools, which teach future leaders, were not ready or teaching what would be needed.

Then, the discussion turned to work and business. Giancarlo, one of the cousins (we always have more cousins than there are cousins), sighed deeply, his frustration evident. "Finding good employees has become an uphill battle," he shared, echoing the sentiment of many around him.

He said that he felt overworked and overwhelmed in his workplace. One of his tasks was to help find enough new employees to fill all the gaps, and he was working so much overtime. The work had to get done, regardless. When he did find people, they either wouldn't come in for an interview or, if hired, would leave sooner than later.

He had tried to get his boss to help, but what was his boss' response to the overwork and finding and keeping employees? "You have to do the extra work. That is what you were hired for: to manage and get the work done. You have the issue, not me."

Giancarlo felt powerless and frustrated.

The older generation at the table, however, had a different take. (Holy shit, was I one in this group? Say it isn't so!)

"In my time, you stuck with a job for life," Marcucio chimed in. "Stability was key." This sparked a lively debate that illustrated a clear generational gap in workplace expectations.

One thread was the defined division between remote and in-person positions as Mario, Marcucio's son, expressed his desire for remote work.

Life with COVID-19 exposed something. The majority of the work in companies moved to remote locations. Now that everything has subsided, many still love staying home and working remotely. Sure, some occupations must work in the business—doctors, nurses, hospital workers, construction workers, etc.—but the younger family members wanted more from their employment. They were choosier with the type of work they accepted. They were looking for benefits from the workplace, whether the benefits were working remotely, money, education, or other perks.

The older generation was split.

In the early days of my business, remote work was a foreign concept. Since then, I've loved the idea of working and coaching from anywhere in the world. Sure, in-person coaching is the best way, though it is not the cheapest.

I explained how I could take the same coaching online and lead a small, intimate group of business owners at a tenth of the cost. This would be good for them and good for me. All I needed was my MacBook and a Wi-Fi connection, and voila! Coaching. All my clients needed was an openness to learn and use our proven foundational tools to build their businesses.

I'm old with a young mind (I'm trying to reconcile my age here) because the even older generation had other ideas and some excellent points. They also had questions. How do the employees get the experience and mentoring they need without live interaction? How do the owners get new ideas if they don't have access to the employees?

My daughters also spoke up and expressed their ideas. They embraced a hybrid model, seamlessly blending old-school ethics with a modern approach.

It was a stark reminder of the evolving landscape and the need for businesses to adapt.

The young almost unanimously said they would not stand for any business or company that could not give them what they wanted. They spoke not in a rah-rah, spoiled way but as young, career-minded families who wanted more from life than their businesses and careers.

The young saw something that the older generation did not.

Life is the reason you work, the reason you have a career, and the reason you start, run, or grow a business.

The older culture was all about work and responsibility. I could see this value in my forefathers' reasons for immigrating here, too. They came to this country with two nickels in their pockets. Work was number one. The family would starve if they didn't work—a perfect incentive.

All sides had a point.

Giancarlo needed good employees—ones who would stay. His higher-ups wanted the work done regardless and wanted the employees to come to work. He could not find them, and when he did, he could not get them in for an interview or keep them long-term once hired.

Michael wanted freedom from what work was to him. He loved to be remote. For him, it was a matter of the job and having more life at home with his wife and two children. He had the opinion that companies needed to offer more than just money. He wanted more from his job.

My daughters loved their careers. Their companies offered remote work, benefits, education, time off, and more freedom from being remote. They would compromise by going to work periodically to network, for meetings, for education, and for learning and sharing new ideas. They have the work ethic of my generation and my parents' generation. Yet, they possess new ways of thinking, living, and working. (I wonder where they learned that value.)

Marcucio and his brother-in-law did not want hybrid *or* remote work. They knew the value of learning from a network of people and gaining experience with on-the-job training. They were the mentors with much-needed expertise and know-how to teach, and let's face it: remote work is, in many cases, a more challenging learning environment. It's not impossible, but it's not as robust.

As I listened and learned from all sides, I did a quick Google search, which revealed a startling statistic: younger workers, on average, stay in a job for just three years.

I shared this insight with the family, highlighting the urgency of rethinking our approach. In my and my parents' generations, if you read a resume that listed many places, you would think something was wrong. We looked for stability and longevity as values. However, traditional expectations are evolving, and employees demand a shift in how employers and owners view employment.

If you read the resumes of this generation, you will see what they gained from each place and what range of experience they can bring to the table. Today, we learn experiences and skills from many places, and this value is becoming the norm.

I offered a solution. If young, career-minded entrepreneurs want freedom, financial professionalism, respect, and to feel part of something bigger, what would happen if you were to create an environment for these beliefs?

To address the employee retention challenge, I proposed a fresh approach—creating an environment that caters to both the workforce's aspirations and the business' goals. This isn't just a theory; it has worked for me. I recounted instances where embracing flexibility and mentorship transformed my employees into loyal, owner-like, empowered employees, not just transient workers.

I continued, "Create an environment in the workplace and remotely that will give the employees success. Owners must build something new. Something that will attract great people."

The owners who cannot make this transition will suffer, just as Giancarlo could not find anyone to fill the employee void. And I will be truthful: most owners will not think in a new way. They own the businesses. They run the companies. Hear them roar.

Owners want more business growth and profits and are looking for good employees.

Employees want to be respected. They want financial rewards. They want professional growth. They want to work remotely, if possible.

Employees want more life. They want more from their companies.

Employees need experience and mentoring, which means more experienced employees need to share their new knowledge and ideas, and owners need to mentor and share their wealth of knowledge. Employees will find ways to get what they need no matter what owners do. They have responsibilities for their families and lives. When there are more opportunities elsewhere, boom, they are gone. They want more from life and more from the company they work for.

Create an environment that supports everyone, financially and professionally, and see what happens.

Let's work with what we have, not wish for what we don't have. Let's live in abundance, not scarcity.

The previous chapters gave you the map and vision. The chapters to come will provide you with a new way to create a professional and financial environment in which everyone can thrive. Your transformation as a leader builds the foundation for this environment.

As the main courses were cleared and our attention focused on the dolce trays teasing us from the corner of the room all night, the discussions started to settle. A moment of reflection lingered in the air as the delicious taste of dolce and sfogliatelle lingered in our mouths.

One truth did emerge: our world is evolving. Our businesses must evolve with it.

We must blend tradition with innovation, from Giancarlo's struggle to find and retain talent to Mario's desire for remote freedom and from my daughters' hybrid approach to Marcucio's old-school ethics. Yet a common thread emerged: the yearning for fulfillment, respect, and growth in both professional and personal spheres.

Harvey S. Firestone said perfectly: "The growth and development of people is the highest calling of leadership."

In conclusion, my favorite part of business and life development is that the formula for growing a business isn't simple. It is where the theory and idea of a career development program meet the reality of taking the time and money to develop the people of your organization.

I see heroes emerge. It was my privilege to nurture my employees into the heroes they aspired to become. By collaborating with and developing them, I discovered the true essence of leadership: the power to transform dreams into realities.

The chapters ahead offer a roadmap for creating an environment where every individual can thrive professionally and financially.

STEP 3:
Developing Systems that Work

"Systems run the Company, People run the Systems, and Leaders lead the People."

—Domenic A Chiarella

To fulfill your vision for a future business and abundant life, we have to look back to the past at the habits and ways of thinking of the entrepreneurial giants that have come before us.

What were their habits?

What paths did they take?

What new way of thinking took them to the top?

I think of giants like Steve Jobs of Apple, Raymond Kroc of Mac-Donald's, Richard Branson of Virgin, and Jeff Bezos of Amazon, to name a few.

Their path to freedom began with a *process*.

There are two ways to operate: you can work in your business as a worker-owner or on your business as a mentoring leader.

The worker-owner is underpaid and overworked, forced to wear all the hats. The leader you have learned to be is a well-paid visionary who has ditched all the working hats and makes a difference. That leader creates the systems, processes, and structure that are most efficient and effective for making the business work.

When you build your business as a leader, you increase your chance of real success and your ability to tap into more free-

dom, creativity, and profits. Like the giants, the more structured your business has, the more financial and life freedoms
you'll experience.

INGREDIENT 7: **The Art of Delegation**

"The system is that there is no system. That doesn't mean we don't have processes. Apple is a very disciplined company, and we have great processes. But that's not what it's about. Process makes you more efficient."

—Steve Jobs

When jarring tomato paste, three things are necessary to have the kind of success we're looking for.

You need a hundred-year-old recipe that outlines the steps for consistently jarring your tomato paste year after year.

You need a leader—in our case, my favorite mom-in-law, Annunziatina, and her mom, Mamma Maria, who have the experience and the vision to recreate that recipe they've used since they were peasants on a farm in Italy during WWII.

You need delicious ingredients: sweet, ripe tomatoes, salt, fresh basil, and mason jars.

Just add love and passion, and voila.

What do jarring tomatoes have to do with your passion for running and growing your business?

When running and growing a business, you also need three things to create the possibility of success (taken from my Strategic Objective—not just money at all costs).

Like the hundred-year-old recipe, you and your company have to find a way to provide excellent service to the client year after year consistently. The business recipe is the steps you take daily to run and grow. The recipe is the systems and processes.

Like Mamma Maria and Annunziatina, you have to have leaders—people like you and me who started the company from humble beginnings and spent years developing the business, cultivating clients, and having the experience.

You need the ingredients: employees hired with values and a hunger for development, people you can mentor who want to be more successful.

Just add love and passion, and voila.

There has always been a catch for business owners as well as Annunziatina and Momma Maria. There is only so much time available to us. One of the most critical, limited resources is time. We only have so many hours in a day, and we can only complete a finite amount of work in those hours. That will never change.

Eventually, like with any excellent service or product people are clamoring for, Annunziatina, my favorite mother-in-law, needed to grow. Her great product was more in demand because her family was growing.

There was a point where she could have done things the same way. She knew that if she worked harder and longer, she could fulfill her family's needs. Yet you know what would happen? The added work and time had to be taken from somewhere else—usually her family life. This is not rocket science. We all know where time gets taken from.

One day, she thought of a better way to do the work *and* spend time with her family. (She may have had a great coach.) She chose a new way.

She:

- Made it a family affair (hired for values and orientation).

- Taught and mentored her team (career development).

- Gave us the steps we needed to follow (developed systems).

We knew our product, who we were making it for, how many jars we would make, and when we needed them (Strategic Objective).

Our shared goals were met year after year, generation after generation because she created an opportunity for her family to help her. Next, we'll learn about that kind of delegation.

🍅 Key Concepts

- **Time Management:** Time is a finite resource. Strategic actions and delegation are essential, encouraging leaders to prioritize tasks and empower others.

- **Team-Building and Leadership:** *A sole proprietor's and a leader's mindsets* are different; if you want to build great teams, you must guide them with effective leadership.

- **Understanding Operations:** Effective leadership first requires understanding organizational purposes and their impact on clients and the company. Developing a Playbook enables leaders to align processes and create consistency across teams.

- **Operations Manual as a Guide:** Consolidating the entire operation into a comprehensive manual provides a centralized resource for employees—a one-stop shop for clarity, consistency, and alignment.

- **The Art of Delegation:** Delegation is a strategic soft skill that enables leaders to leverage their team members' capabilities, alleviate time constraints, and focus on essential activities.

CHAPTER 21:
Systems Run the Company

"We need to work together to optimize the system as a whole, not to seek to optimize separate pieces...optimizing separate pieces destroys the effectiveness of the whole. For the organization to work well as a whole, the components must work together."

—Brian Joiner

In 2011, I took a leap from running a creative, exciting, twenty-seven-year, top three percent property landscape/snow removal management partnership to creating an exciting coaching and mentoring organization.

I went from leading, mentoring, strategizing, and creating robust systems and structures for my organization to showing business owners like you exactly how to become extraordinary leaders who build thriving organizations and have the freedom to live extraordinary lives.

Whether from a speaking stage and blogging at *The Art of Life*, hosting live workshops on business and life, or coaching one-on-one clients worldwide, I have enjoyed guiding others toward exponential growth and helping creative entrepreneurs find extraordinary success in their lives.

I help you build your business around your life rather than living your life that revolves around business.

This didn't happen by handing out systems and letting them rip. First, the two keys of leadership and employee development must be in place for a business and, more importantly, for me, a life transformation to happen in response to systems.

When we start with strategic work in leadership and employee development, the final piece of the business puzzle—system development—works—and it *really* works.

Systems Free Our Focus

The secret is out. How do the best of the best of the best do it?

Their systems and structures run their companies, period.

All the giants, the highly successful, the great coaches, and the grand pooh-bahs say the same thing: systems, systems, systems.

They are correct, and you were too. You instinctively knew that developing systems in your company would give you growth, profits, and freedom. System Development *is* the answer to your prayers.

System Development is where you will create, develop, and implement systems, processes, templates, and flows that can run your business consistently and effectively.

Hear me out, though. You can create, develop, and implement to your heart's content. But to have these systems, processes, flows, and templates work consistently and effectively, you need your people to be able to run them.

That is the catch, the pivot, the connection.

You are not attracting and keeping "just any" employees. You now know that you need employees with your values and who are professionally developed within your career development programs. These people are able and willing to run your systems and processes.

But wait; there's more.

There is another catch, pivot, connection: leader development comes first.

Before your employees were capable of running those systems, you had to have rock-solid foundations for your business and be thoroughly grounded in your life. You named what you value in your life and created your business to satisfy your Purpose in Life.

That's when the power of systems comes alive.

Transitioning from solely managing the company to delegating tasks and implementing systems marks a crucial turning point, not just in workload management but in ensuring consistent quality.

Like a hundred-year-old recipe for tomato paste consistently providing excellence, businesses need systems and processes to run the company, people to run the systems, and leaders to lead the people.

Likewise, just as Annunziatina brought her family together to assist in the jarring process, a business leader must build a team of value-driven people who share the company's values and vision and then delegate tasks to these trusted team members.

One result will be releasing the leader's time burden. The second will be empowering employees with owner-like powers. They can now take ownership of their responsibilities and contribute to the company's success.

Great businesses depend on systems and processes for every detail, from sales processes to production and servicing clients, how you hire, and the steps to pay employees, vendors, and taxes. Yet the mere mention of "letting the systems run the company" sends shivers down the spines of many owners. Creating the systems isn't as challenging as having the people run the systems consistently. The reality is it will take work to create the automatic flows that you dream of having.

Annunziatina and Mamma Maria successfully changed their approach to jarring tomato paste; businesses can achieve the same by embracing delegation, systemization, and strategic planning.

I get incredibly excited about system development, not only about creating systems but also about implementing them in a way that works. The tools and interdepartmental flows connect the people who make up the company, and this last section showcases the positive impact such tools can have on owners and employees. When systems run the company, and people run the systems, day-to-day tasks can become automatic.

The beauty?

It frees up the leader's time to think more about what is essential—the company's strategies and systems—instead of getting caught up in the tedious or mundane. It frees up the employees' time to think about what is essential—the client—instead of being caught up in the tedious or mundane.

Let Your People Run the Systems

Let's assume you have given your people the systems, processes, result-oriented positions, vision, values, and some of the best mentoring available.

What will surprise you at this stage is that they will welcome the responsibility of running the company.

Together, my partner and I created something unique in our organization.

His superpowers were his sales and networking abilities.

My superpower was creating synergy between systems and processes, technology, and people.

I managed collaboratively and often marveled at how the employees took responsibility for their positions and teams. Of course, shit still hits the fan sometimes, as it always will. I knew, and they knew, that we would solve the issues first and foremost and then return to determine how to fix what happened.

We were a learning and teaching organization, so after we first looked at fixing the problem to serve the client better, we moved to mentor to ensure it would not happen again. Let's face it: most issues are client-related, and in those situations, there is little time or place to verbally slap someone for making a mistake. (Thinking back on all my mistakes, if a slap were the answer, I would be a dead man.)

When employees feel safe from the owner's wrath, it is easier for them to learn, stretch, and grow into leaders.

My motto became their learned motto:

Fix the issue immediately.

Come back ASAP to look at what happened.

Update the system or mentor a misunderstood system/flow.

Move forward.

You may remember the shit-hit-the-fan issue in Chapter 18, when we discussed a Sunday night invoicing and client profile issue between a partner and a new employee, Lucy.

One partner attempted to solve the issue his way, while I followed my process by mentoring Lucy.

Was it a system breakdown that needed to be fixed? No. The system was solid.

Was the issue related to education? Yes. The next step would be education.

Was the issue related to people's communication? Also, a yes. We needed to work on how work was communicated.

Was it a position issue? No.

Was it a value issue? No.

Notice that I did not start with the employee. (Although my partner certainly did!) I started with the system's steps: education, communication, position, and, lastly, mentoring with values.

If it had been a system issue, I would have spent time updating the system, documenting the change, and teaching it to the entire team.

Instead, I needed to solve the people/communication issue immediately, so I calmed the situation with everyone involved: partner, new employee, and office. I spoke to my partner and explained the need for communication and respect. He apologized and understood that respect and communication were our values. I talked to Lucy, asked her to reconsider staying, and asked if I could show her the filing system.

Since Lucy was still in orientation, I had a sneaky idea that the real issue was education. When I showed her how the system worked and what flowed between departments, Lucy immediately had a "V8 moment." She had an educational misunderstanding of the system, saw that I cared, and appreciated that I had addressed and resolved my partner's outburst.

I never made it to the point of assessing her position or values. If an employee had our values but was not in the position they should be in, we could help them to a better position in the company. If not, like David's different values in chapter 15, the last resort would be to help them find another company to work for.

Too many leaders "solve" issues with what should be the last resort. They make the employee the problem. Those leaders start with the outburst toward the employee, sometimes going to the extreme and eliminating them quickly.

I disagree with this approach. I made many mistakes, but I found my superpower when I learned to let go of "I am boss; hear me roar." In return, my employees trusted me and felt safe. They would come to me with any issue, knowing that we would get to the heart of the problem and work on how not to let it happen again.

The hardest part about letting your people run the systems is letting go of the feeling that you are the only one allowed to make mistakes.

Thanks to your blood, sweat, and tears, the company is where it is today. You and your team have the tools to take it to another level. If you can hold on to that "entity of one" identity, you will become the organization's kryptonite.

You can grow into something more.

When I ask owners why they want to grow, they rarely know what "growth" means. Revenue can grow, yes. Systems can grow. Employees can grow. The organization can grow. You can grow.

Growth is intertwined, depending on how much a leader can grow.

Releasing control may feel like the final frontier, a place no one has gone before. However, the most successful leaders and companies, including myself, have gone to that frontier before you.

Once I understood what it meant to let my people run the systems—to let them make mistakes, fix issues, learn, and move forward—my time in my company became the most creative and energizing years of my life and business.

CHAPTER 22:
Build the Playbook

"Wisdom is the power to put our time and our knowledge to the proper use."

—Thomas J. Watson

It's impossible to have all the information at any given moment. Do your homework and due diligence. Seek input from your team. Remember, you'll never know everything. Leap—move forward. When new information inevitably arises, make the necessary adjustments and keep progressing.

Imagine extracting a hundred-year-old tomato paste recipe from an Italian mom, Mamma Maria, and her daughter, Annunziatina. They've perfected their craft over decades, and food is their life's purpose. If they are used to getting it done all by themselves, how will they trust others enough to give them the reins? After all, it is their creation, their money, their time, and their reputation that is on the line. (A little secret about Italian moms and grandmoms: food is everything to them; it is their purpose in life. You mess with them, and you mess with your life.)

Similarly, as a business owner, your company's success depends on the intricate knowledge stored in your mind. How do you ensure that others can duplicate your success?

How do you remove all the strategies, systems, and steps from the mind of an owner who is used to doing everything alone? How can you ensure that the employees will follow the systems consistently? How do you know they will run the company like the owner would?

After all, it is your creation, money, time, and reputation on the line.

My experience (and persistence), as well as the advice of the giants, suggests it's not only possible but also well worth the effort to document what you know so that others can follow.

Building the Systems Playbook

A Systems Playbook is your business' blueprint, ensuring employees understand and follow the same procedures to achieve consistent results. This is crucial for scaling operations, maintaining quality, and freeing up your time for strategic growth.

To lead effectively, you need to grasp the function of everything you and your team members do, the timing and impact of everything, and who is responsible for each function.

Per usual, I will not sugarcoat this process. Building a Playbook that includes the processes, systems, templates, and flows the employees will use to run your company will take time. Think of the countless tasks you've handled alone—sales, scheduling, ordering, proposals, contracts, etc.

It is overwhelming and time-consuming to do so many tasks. I know that teaching someone every step of those tasks is even more daunting, but we are embarking on a journey to streamline your efforts as you become a better leader. It begins with self-awareness and a keen understanding of your daily operations.

I promise it will not take all of Annunziatina's one hundred years. In my organization, it took three years.

At the beginning of my growth, I was figuring it all out without a guide. Once I hired coaches, they kept me on my game. My new leadership position required me to build and implement something I had never done, one step at a time. Slowly, I figured out how to document what my partner and I did, create a system from those one-page documents, implement the systems, and train one agonizing step after another.

You have a guide for this system development.

This process has taken less than a year for every organization for which I've had the honor of coaching.

We will follow the KISS concept (keep it simple, stupid): As you do your daily functions and processes, get them from your head and onto paper. Start with whatever you're responsible for, and build out from there.

Chronicling each detail of your daily operations will allow you to delegate tasks more effectively and shed light on the patterns and problems lurking under the surface. When I started documenting my processes, I used a simple spiral notebook. It was always by my side so I could capture every detail. This humble start grew into a sophisticated Operations Manual that revolutionized my business operations.

Build Your Playbook

- **Choose Your Tools:** Whether a spiral notebook or a digital platform like Word, Google Docs, Dropbox, or iCloud, pick one you'll regularly use to start collecting notes about your tasks and processes.

- **Identify Categories:** Create a table of contents with sections like Sales, Production, Accounting, Marketing, Strategic, Financial, etc., reflecting the areas you want to develop and delegate.

- **Categorize Your Tasks:** Assign each task or process to its respective area. For example, sales-related tasks go under the Sales section.

- **Document Your Tasks:** For each task, create a one-page, step-by-step list with essential details:

- O Task name

- O Position responsible

- O Resources required

- O Task description

- O The result of the task

- O Steps to perform the task

Every time you do something in your business (creating a proposal, for example), give it a system or process name (e.g., Proposal Process) and write it under the area where it belongs (Sales). Proposals, contracts, client contacts, etc., go into Sales. Work orders, schedule boards, and material handling go into Production. Invoicing, payable, payroll, and filing go into Accounting.

Let's use the first meeting of your orientation program as an example.

Chapter 17 discussed the materials required for new employees just beginning orientation. One of these is the New Employee Packet, filled with various forms and agreements to be signed and kept on file for HR purposes and to meet state and federal employment requirements. This interdepartmental system can be documented in two categories: HR and the specific department's orientation process.

HR would gather the documents for the New Employee Packet, turn them over to the mentor guiding orientation, and then file them properly once they have been returned. The mentor would have a matching process: They would obtain the New Employee Packet from HR, help the new employee complete each form, and return the packet to HR as soon as they are done.

Within the System Playbook, that process might look something like this:

1. Task Name: New Employee Packet

2. Task Description: This packet contains all the forms the new employee must complete for local, state, and federal taxes, insurance, payroll, etc.

3. Position Responsible for the Task: Department Manager assigned to Orientation

4. Resources Available to Do the Task: The New Employee Packet should include the following forms: Employment Application, Form W4: Federal Withholding Certificate, Form [Your State]-W4: State Exemption Certificate, Medical Insurance Accept/Decline Form, Authorization for Direct Deposit, Confidentiality Agreement, 401(k) Enrollment Form, Profit-Sharing Plan Enrollment Form

5. Steps to Do the Task: Obtain a New Employee Packet from HR, complete the documents with the new employee, and return the completed documents to HR.

6. Clear Result of the Task: A packet template with all the documents needed for all incoming employees. The first page has an outline you can follow and check off as completed.

The department would follow a similar process, with slightly different language depending on which role is responsible and what they do with the material afterward. Theirs would be filed under their department.

As you document each task, please keep it to a one-page, bulleted, step-by-step list. Include any diagrams, charts, or images that make the process easier to visualize. If you can't write it, you can't teach it.

When transitioning from a command-and-control owner to a mentoring leader, the systems you document may not be the most effective. That's okay. These Playbooks are living documents that can and should be updated as your systems improve and your company grows. You can also make this a collaborative process, with input from various departments and regular updates from those following the processes.

As the song goes, "This is how we do it." This is the cornerstone of your System Playbook, the bible of your business. Creating this playbook is how you get everything out of your head and down on paper. It is one of the tools that will help you in your leadership journey and practice effective delegation.

All the work we've done so far has led to this step. You had to get clear on your purposes, strategy, and values. Your hiring is now aligned with people to clear positions, oriented to them, and focused on helping them develop a leader-like mindset so they can thoroughly and reliably take responsibility for their positions. Combined with a System Playbook, each task turns delegation into a structured process for you to follow instead of an uncertain experiment.

Train, monitor, mentor, rinse, and repeat.

Rounding Out the Operations Manual

A System Playbook will be part of an Operations Manual. This manual combines all those pieces into one bible-like guide that supports each employee in their role and keeps everyone on the same page. A robust Operations Manual includes the vision, values, processes, workflows, and mentorship opportunities employees can expect to participate in.

This can be accomplished by compiling everything we've named so far:

- Your Strategic Objective is the map and the vision for the company
- Your Company Values as a long-term why you exist as a company
- An Organizational Chart, including the workflows between departments and the specific skills needed for roles within the department and company
- The Employee's Position Agreement
- The Systems Playbook for that position, with detailed processes for their various tasks
- A more general Systems Playbook for the company, for a broader understanding of the systems the role will interact with
- An Employee Handbook, including details about the structured training opportunities the employee will be able to expect and take advantage of

Eventually, these documents will become the backbone of the company's systems, eliminating ambiguity about who does what, when, and how. The people who run the systems can go into autopilot mode, making their results consistent and freeing their creative minds to streamline those processes even more or handle new client requests as soon as they arise.

CHAPTER 23:
The Art of
Delegation

"When you delegate tasks, you create followers. When you delegate authority, you create leaders."

—Craig Groeschel

One Sunday, after our traditional pasta dinner, my family and I went for a drive. As it was getting dark, I made a bonus suggestion that never failed: "Let's get some ice cream!"

"Yeah! Daddy is the best!" (I knew it, but I always liked to hear it.)

My wife smiled from the front seat, and my mother-in-law, who loves sitting behind me, gave her usual calm nod. It reminded me of Clemenza from *The Godfather* and his famous line, "Leave the gun. Take the cannoli."

As we headed toward Rich Farms, our favorite homemade ice cream haunt, my phone rang. It was one of my top clients.

I pulled over to take the call. My wife and mother-in-law exchanged glances, knowing this wouldn't be quick.

Even though it was getting dark, I could see my wife's leery eyes.

I flipped open my phone.

"You need a project done? Of course, Ms. T. You're having a party on Monday afternoon? Of course, Ms. T. It's no problem. What do you need?"

I listened and mumbled out loud as I took down all the information.

I was smiling to myself. I was going to impress my family with my new delegation skills.

"When do you need this to get done? Tonight! You will contact the guards and tell them we will work late into the night? Okay. Let me get right on it."

I got off the phone with my client and called all my employees. For the next few minutes, I "delegated" on the side of the road. My wife looked at me—*really* looked at me like only a loving wife can.

She said, "What the hell are you doing on a Sunday night? Why are you doing all the managing? Tell her you will be there early in the morning. Are you going to drive to her house now? We are going to the ice cream farm. You are crazy!"

Just as everything was set in motion, my client called again to cancel for the night. She wanted the crew there in the morning instead.

"Of course, Ms. T. Good night. See you in the morning."

I wrapped up the project setup and turned to my wife, expecting some kudos for the new delegation skills I was working on with my executive coach. Instead, all I saw was her glare. My mother-in-law's eyes met mine in the rearview mirror, and I could almost hear, "Hello, Pauli."

My wife, rightfully angry, explained that what I was doing wasn't proper delegation. It was micromanagement.

I was stunned.

She was right, of course. Delegation isn't just about assigning tasks. It's about entrusting your team with responsibilities and empowering them to act.

What I did that night was merely "getting the job done." My wife's wisdom hit me hard: "You are still doing all the work. They are just following your commands."

I realized I was afraid that delegating tasks meant giving up control. This incident reshaped my management style.

Suppose you choose the right tasks to delegate to the right person and equip them with the necessary resources. In that case, your company will succeed more than if you tried to do everything yourself.

Simple? Yes. Easy? Hardly.

I received something precious besides a hot fudge chocolate chip ice cream sundae that evening. It was a new perspective. I realized:

- There is a difference between delegation and micromanagement. Proper delegation involves entrusting my team with responsibilities, not just tasks.

- I must empower my team by equipping them with the resources and authority they need to succeed.

- Trust is leadership. Effective delegation requires trust and a shift from a sole proprietorship mindset to a leadership mindset.

- Sustainable growth is only possible when I let go of the illusion of self-reliance and embrace team management.

- A leader's ability to delegate effectively isn't just a managerial skill; it is the alignment of values, cultivation of a shared vision, and mentorship invested in the team.

Better Together

The incident with my partner and my new employee, Lucy, was a turning point in my leadership journey. I knew I needed to be a calm and confident leader and ensure the new value-hired employees understood that we meant what we said about our culture.

Everyone was watching me.

I realized that effective delegation isn't about relinquishing control but empowering each employee to take ownership of their role. It's about building trust and providing the necessary resources and support for my team to thrive.

Think about your approach to delegation.

Are you genuinely empowering your team or still holding onto control?

How do you get employees to do the things you need or want them to do?

A simple answer is that you can't.

It doesn't work that way. You cannot get employees to do what they do not want to do.

Then, how do you harness the power of employees?

The Pyramid of Success Framework is the answer to these questions. It is the synergy of Leaders, Employees, and Systems. It created success in my four organizations and the companies I coach.

The bottom of the pyramid is the systems that run your organization. This is the foundation. The right side is the network of employees responsible for running the systems. The left side is the owners who lead the employees with vision, strategy, and culture.

To learn more about the Pyramid of Success, click here or put the link in your browser for bonus material on my website: TomatoPasteLeadership.com/bonus.

What do owners need to do to make this organization great? Jim Rohn states, "For things to change, you have to change."

What role does a leader play in an organization? *You have to change* from an owner-worker to an owner-leader.

You bring people together around a shared vision, foster a culture where education and learning are fundamental, and mentor others to create an environment where everyone thrives. You include well-defined positions and systems. Now, you empower your team with the tools and opportunities they need to succeed.

The company forms a collective mind when people recognize that they need one another to succeed. This enables them to bond around a common identity and stick together to achieve collective goals.

In my experience as an owner and a coach, I have found that a great team does not consist of the brightest, most experienced employees. It is a collection of minds and ideas that focus on common goals.

Remember the pre-snow-event meeting in the preface?

It was art because of how the *team* performed. It was how the group achieved a common goal, creating the most profitable, effective, and client-satisfying event that year.

Do you remember when Mina asked me, "What are you doing in this meeting?" It still puts a smile on my face.

I learned to smile when someone asked what would happen if I couldn't work due to an unforeseeable situation. How would the company continue without me? My answer became, "You can stop me. You can even stop one of the employees. But you cannot stop all of us. We are a true team."

When I became comfortable not being the brightest bulb in the bunch or being the center of knowledge, I became a better leader. I had my role. I is an engineer. I loved system development. I loved to take people, departments, systems, flows, and software and make them into art. I savored it. Yet that role was part of a team.

What was my role in that meeting? In the organization? One role I played well was creating the future strategy and Organizational Chart and building the process to unlock this collective intelligence.

Another role was showing my pride in the team. I aligned everyone around a common goal, carved out a unique role for each member, and taught everyone to recognize that they needed one another to succeed.

You don't need to have the best single-owner thinking. You need to have *team* thinking. Then, you will be unstoppable.

The next time you're faced with a task, consider who on your team is best suited for it and how you can support them in taking it on.

Start today by identifying one task you can delegate.

Equip the person with the resources needed and trust them to deliver.

Observe the process and learn from the experience.

Take the time to build a team process and an organizational system to unlock your collective intelligence—and then unleash it.

As a leader, your role is to guide and mentor your team, not to do everything yourself. Embrace the power of delegation, and watch your business grow and thrive with a team that feels trusted, empowered, and proud of their work.

INGREDIENT 8:
An Environment of Trust

"One of the great sources of frustration and rancor in relationships is that we tend to want to change some behavior in the other person that annoys or hurts us. They often resist this change, and we become even more irritated…when we connect with others based on shared values and vulnerability, it is much easier to set goals and agree on compromises that will work for both parties."

—Steven C. Hayes, *A Liberated Mind*

After reading Seth Godin's *Linchpin*, I asked my three mentors, "What kind of leader am I?" I wasn't on the front lines, boastful, or in need of the limelight. I *was* willing to learn and develop myself.

One mentor called me a quiet leader who works in the background without boasting and needing the limelight. The other called me a linchpin because you don't have to be in the front to lead. Leading is more than ego. It is more than the spotlight.

Dad said, "You are the glue that would be missed if removed from the mix. Don't negate your contribution."

I liked that.

Leadership transformation is akin to creating a masterpiece and becoming the organization's linchpin and glue. The leader's transformation into a mentor and visionary creates a ripple effect, fostering growth at all levels.

It clicked when I read the above quote in Steven Hayes' book *A Liberated Mind*.

"One of the great sources of frustration and rancor in relation-ships is that we tend to want to change some behavior in the other person that annoys or hurts us. They often resist this change, and we become even more irritated."

Remember the roundtable conversation when I said, "I do not believe you can make anyone come to the table. You cannot make anyone do anything."

Steven Hayes knows you can't make any employee do anything. When building or leading a team, you are often irritated if you focus on the wrong areas, such as trying to change others' be-haviors. "WTF are they resisting?"

With a computer engineering background, I am well-versed in creating systems and flows. System development came natu-rally to me and was the easiest part of growing the company.

The most challenging part of leading a company and having employees run it is effectively implementing systems, people, hardware, and software.

Key questions may come to mind when you are thinking about how systems work seamlessly:

- Did the systems help you? In my case, yes.

- Did they make you more effective? Yes.

- Did they last in a command-and-control environment? No. They caused more confusion because something was missing.

- Did adding employees who shared your values help? Yes.

- Did it make work better? Yes.

- Did the old-guard employees buy in? More no than yes.

- Did the old guard cause more confusion? Yes.

I realized something was missing—and the piece missing in the Pyramid of Success Framework was me. (Say it isn't so!)

I needed better leadership skills. I needed better tools.

When I added strategy, values, and positions, the systems started to work. But beware: even with all those tools and realizations, fear of losing control often shapes how we lead with them. Here, I propose an unconventional perspective of control: the idea that the owner works for management, and management works for the team.

In the following chapters, we will delve deeper into these concepts. I will provide practical steps and real-life examples to illustrate how you can transform your leadership approach and fully trust your team.

By embracing these principles and integrating the tools we've discussed, you will create a dynamic and resilient organization that thrives on trust, collaboration, and continuous growth.

This is the linchpin section of the book.

🍅 Key Concepts

- **Thriving Upside Down:** This environment emerges when traditional power structures are flipped, fostering a culture where everyone plays a vital role.

- **Collaboration over Hierarchy:** Shift from traditional hierarchical structures to a collaborative, Circular Organizational Chart that prioritizes employee well-being and satisfaction and improves overall organizational performance.

- **Create an Inclusive Workplace Culture:** Foster an inclusive and positive workplace culture that understands the organization thrives when all employees thrive.

- **Innovate Through Collaboration:** Innovation emerges when the entire company works together.

- **Cultivate Servant Leadership:** Support and uplift team members through servant leadership principles.

CHAPTER 24:
Trust Your People

"Communication—the human connection—is the key to personal and career success."

—Paul J. Meyer

A few months after the Clemenza Ice Cream Caper, one of my clients requested a project that would truly test our "service the client, period" value.

We serviced this twenty-five-acre farm three times weekly. It boasted apple orchards, flower and vegetable gardens, topiaries, a horse stable, and more. It is a breathtaking estate and my personal favorite.

We were at the end of one of our weeks, all looking forward to heading into a religious holiday weekend, Easter Sunday. That day was Good Friday, and even though the workers were devout and it was a significant religious day, they wanted to work. The offer of triple time for workers who stuck around that day was not just about money; it resonated with the family values we shared with our employees. Many of our employees, immigrants from Mexico, related to my Italian upbringing. They worked tirelessly for their families in the US and Mexico, and the extra pay that day meant more they could take or send home.

As we worked through the final cleanup and paperwork, the client came out, walked the property, expressed appreciation, and conversed politely. I watched her compliment the workers as she strolled: "Thank you for this. Thank you for that. This looks amazing. Domenic, your employees are very hard workers."

It was evident that our service-oriented values resonated with her as well.

As we packed up, she approached me with a request. Pointing at the window that covered the whole side of the sunroom, she said, "Domenic, I am hosting a luncheon in my sunroom, and you can see this area through the beautiful picture window. I would love my friends to look out the sunroom window and enjoy a sea of white daisies or yellow pansies surrounded by English boxwood hedges."

She continued, "I am also looking for more grandeur inside the sunroom. I can see four large, aged terracotta pots with hanging Spanish moss and four-foot arborvitaes in each room corner. I would love to see a medley of flowers and pots on the opposite side of the luncheon room."

I pulled out my estimate template and took notes as she continued.

Two large pots, aged? Yes, of course, we can age the terracotta pots.

Four-foot arborvitae trees? Uh-huh.

Spanish moss? Yes, we can get that.

Colorful flowers in the garden outside the picture window? About 1,000 plants would suffice.

White daisies surrounding the silver ball? They're hard to find this time of year, but I know one of our greenhouses may have just what we want.

A rack of pots and colorful flowers in the room? I know just what is needed.

"Of course. No problem."

My Spidey sense tingled, though. On high alert, I asked, "When would you like this project done?"

She smiled and said she wanted it done overnight!

My initial thoughts raced through logistical challenges—material availability, worker availability, and the timely completion of a substantial project. On top of those logistics, it was 4:00 p.m. on Friday of Easter weekend, when many greenhouses, nurseries, and pottery places were closed.

I shared only a few details with her, anticipating the potential obstacle of working all night. She was unfazed. "Thank you, Domenic. I am looking forward to the results."

Watching my client walk into her estate, I embarked on this seemingly impossible task.

I had a team of like-minded individuals with unified values and efficient systems. I trusted my team and the systems we'd meticulously developed. I knew the three keys were firmly in place: efficient systems, well-trained individuals, and a collaborative management approach.

It wasn't just about the physical work but also about fostering an environment where every team member felt trusted, safe, and empowered to take owner-like initiative. They knew their efforts contributed to a collective masterpiece.

As we navigated the challenges, I took a moment to capture the estimate details. I then uploaded them to my ace-in-the-hole right hand, Mina, setting a chain reaction in motion.

Everyone was aligned with the plan, from Mina's paperwork flow and coordination of paperwork distribution to the production manager, was aligned with the plan. Julio orchestrated the project, calling in supervisors and coordinating with people and materials. Mick organized all the equipment and trucks. Mina and Julio coordinated with the owners of our nursery vendors.

The wheels turned on and on, with timely updates for me. (They like to impress me!)

The team spent the night doing this last-minute project.

The project was a success. The client was thrilled, and the luncheon went splendidly.

This experience went beyond a mere project; it exemplified how a value-driven company operates. We set up efficient systems, hired and trained value-oriented individuals, and worked collectively to live up to those values.

Reflecting on how we worked that day compared to past challenges, I felt a profound sense of accomplishment. The Spidey-sense feeling wasn't dread. It was muscle memory—memories of growth and evolution. The team's success mirrored my journey from command and control to collaborative leadership.

As we wrapped up, I couldn't help but marvel at how this seemingly impossible task brought out the best in our team. It wasn't just about completing a project; it was about a collective mindset shift, a testament to the strength of our values and the power of collaborative leadership. It was art, even more beautiful than the Spanish moss, aged terracotta pots, and flowers. Our collaborative management method turned a challenging client request into something we were all proud to be part of, and the completed masterpiece exceeded expectations.

This is how a value-driven company lives, plays, and works.

Value-oriented employees are happy to take owner-like initiative to manage complex projects without you, but only when you give them that owner-like ability.

CHAPTER 25:
Put Your People First

"Genius starts with individual brilliance. It requires a singular vision. But executing it often entails working with others. Innovation is a team sport. Creativity is a collaborative endeavor."

—Walter Isaacson, *Leonardo da Vinci*

The extraordinary speaker from that conference and his "shhhhhhhh" had warned us that we were a facade unless we were willing to get our hands dirty and do something about it. He helped me understand that we could be like many companies that give a great image of success or choose to do something different.

I wanted something different. I wanted success in the truest sense of the word.

I knew I also needed to grow the company behind the scenes as we worked our little Italian hearts out. I did not want that BS values-painted-on-the-wall facade.

I knew I could not use this facade to "sell" our company as an excellent workplace. Employees can see an owner's true nature. Reality had to back up those "we believe in our employees' success" claims.

Our environment needed to change.

The Upside-Down Organizational Chart

In the business world, we often work within the confines of a traditional hierarchy. Departments are neatly stacked, with each level serving the one above. But the kind of leadership we're growing toward flips that script.

Picture this: the owner, instead of presiding at the top of the charts, becomes the one working for management, making sure each person in that "level" has everything they need to succeed. They set the Strategic Objective to provide managers with a visionary outlook, offer cultural mentorship, and ensure the entire team has the training and support they need for optimal performance.

Likewise, the management team focuses on the supervisors, offering situational guidance, system training, and developmental opportunities. Then, the teams themselves are fully supported, trained, and trusted to do what's necessary to serve the client exceptionally well.

When the Organizational Chart is inverted, the roles traditionally on the bottom are at the top. Now, the people traditionally on the bottom are at the top—the most important because they serve the client. The owners, CEOs, and bosses are at the bottom, crucial to employee satisfaction.

It's my turn to throw the Bullshit Card because I can hear you: "Domenic, I am all about the employees."

I work with too many business owners and a few too many partners who tell me they are employee-centric and that the owners work for the employees. Bullshit, I say.

It's easy to imagine the client at the top. I've always placed the client at the forefront of everything in the business. When I embraced this upside-down approach that values service, mentorship, and development from the bottom up, I also learned to extend the client-first philosophy to everyone connected to the organization.

Whether a department, vendor, subcontractor, associate, or professional, "service the client, period" meant treating every role with the same client-focused approach.

Collaborative Management with a Circular Organizational Chart

Once you're willing to turn the hierarchy upside down, a beautiful new possibility opens: the Circular Organizational Chart, where different departments can take center stage in any business cycle based on their unique contributions.

For example, during the sales phase, the sales department takes the center position as they strive to create solid proposals and secure contracts. As contracts are finalized, the spotlight shifts to the service/production department responsible for delivering on promises and satisfying clients. Of course, the accounting department steps into the limelight whenever it's time to seamlessly manage vendor payments, employee payroll, taxes, and other financial matters.

Consider the magic that happens when there is no defined top *or* bottom. Every department becomes vital in its moment while remaining intricately linked to the success of the others. This collaboration is art, where each department is viewed with the importance and attention we typically provide clients.

Something remarkable happens when employees and departments treat each other the way they treat clients. For instance, if Production is viewed as a client of Sales, Sales doesn't just create contracts based on arbitrary demands. Instead, they craft contracts efficiently and thoughtfully, ensuring Production has everything it needs to succeed.

In turn, Sales serves Production by taking contracts and carefully providing all the necessary information for Production to perform at its best. Then, Production becomes a client of Accounting, supplying work orders and critical details with the same precision and care for Accounting to perform its best.

A culture of mutual support emerges when each department treats others as internal clients. Instead of working in silos or competing for resources, teams collaborate with the same dedication, energy, and focus they would offer to external clients. This ensures the entire organization is aligned to serve its external clients better, creating a stronger, more cohesive business.

This is what I know is Art.

This paradigm shift makes everyone a manager and makes them think like owners. A circular structure recognizes every department's importance, cultivating a synergy where no one is more crucial than anyone else. This requires you to trust that your systems can run the company and your value-oriented people can run those systems, taking all that pressure to control off your shoulders.

This can be the most frightening step of all. You will have to give up the power.

I will tell you, hands down, that what seems like giving up your control and power gives you more control and power as the ego and illusion fall away. Then, the real growth begins, the real-time freedom begins, and the real magic begins.

When employees know and feel you trust them, they will also trust you. As they feel safer making empowered decisions, they will contribute more to the company—and the more owner-like powers they have, the more strategic those contributions will become.

Client-Centered Mindset Training

When I worked with Lucy in Chapter 18, my values of education and systems were on display. I also showed her that I trusted her. You might think I wanted Lucy to trust me first, but I went first. I trusted that she could learn, so I gave her an environment to facilitate that learning and made it safe for her to fail on her way to success.

The reward for creating trust and safety is abundance.

My goal of having more freedom was realized one step at a time. My values of client-centered employees and a culture of career development helped her excel in her position and thrive financially and professionally.

As our mentoring sessions continued, I watched as a star was born. Lucy was one of the best employees I have ever had in that position and a vital part of the solid and unstoppable team we built in the accounting department.

Still, I can only reflect on my organization's wins and challenges while turning the Organizational Chart upside down. No matter how much my story makes sense to you, letting go of the tasks, mindset, and hierarchy that got you to this point can be downright frightening.

You have a lot to face. For owners still trying to keep it all together, trusting systems and employees can feel like a crazy risk. Excluding employees from this equation leads to system failures. Not the other way around.

Your systems keep the results you have always produced. These systems keep the company results in check, as your people keep the systems in check. There's nothing to fear here but the loss of your ego.

If your identity is defined by your place at the top of an Organizational Chart, it will be hard for you to turn that chart upside down—much less trust a circular system to ebb and flow with the needs of the business.

I have coached many companies where the owner identity has and keeps this "I am boss; hear me roar" ego. They believe they know all. I will tell you, it is what kept me and will keep these ego owners from stepping into the environment that allows a business to thrive.

That's not to say their fears are imagined. Trust is never without risk. Whether experiencing rapid growth or barely surviving, running a business can feel fragile. You are the one holding the bag.

Trust is a daring venture that propels us beyond the borders of fear, fostering an environment where everyone in the business survives and thrives. It's a journey not without pitfalls, but the rewards are more than worth it.

CHAPTER 26:
Overcoming Fear and Misalignment

"Delegating work works, provided the one delegating works, too."

—Robert Half

Systems alone were insufficient if the environment didn't evolve. I needed to develop as a leader—alongside the foundational changes we made to our systems and people.

As I mentor my clients' leadership growth, I see something we all experience: fear of the unknown and change. This keeps us stuck.

Fear and crazy-ass assumptions.

Fear had kept me from examining my values and how misaligned our business had become for a long time.

Fear had kept me from building the value-oriented teams I needed.

Fear had kept me from letting go enough to practice the art of delegation.

I had assumed that profits would give me more time for my family.

I had assumed that new systems would make the employees think and act in a new way.

I feared that I wouldn't get what I wanted if they *didn't* act differently after all those changes. It was my responsibility to make it all happen.

To overcome those fears, I had to learn and evolve as a leader before I could trust my people, the systems we built for them to run, and the values underneath it all.

Education as a Catalyst

Let me show you what happens in one of our system education sessions.

We were in the middle of an educational session on work order invoice flow systems. This process touched the sales, production, and invoicing departments, and everyone from each department who used the system was in attendance. I always loved the energy these sessions provided, physically uniting every department in one room. It was an interactive assessment of our internal processes, not just a lecture.

We were having interdepartmental challenges with the sales-to-production flow. As we progressed through each department's role in the work order process, an unexpectedly wonderful experience surfaced.

A visibly frustrated foreman, Esteban, bolted up, waving a piece of paper in hand, and said, "Take a look at this work order. It tells me to 'build a wall.' I don't know where to build it, what materials I need, or when it needs to be done."

He paused, looked around the room, and ensured he had everyone's attention. Then he continued, "Now I have to look for all these things and waste my time. I believe I am doing someone else's work. This work has nothing to do with me or my crew completing this project. Where is this information, and why must I figure it out?"

His inquiry echoed a sentiment shared by many: the struggle to perform one's position to excellence while doing others' work before starting one's own.

Holy shit. Let the games begin.

I was smiling on the inside. (Well, a little on the outside.) In this session, I was trying to teach and mentor how to create flows that prevented operational inefficiencies. In other words, how could I get sales to do sales work and production to do production work? How could I make these departments client-centered?

To my surprise, and without hesitation, the executive sales administrator stood up with an unscripted and sincere admission: "Oh, I am so sorry. I did not know how my work affected anyone else. What do you need on the work order? How can I do this better?"

I was shocked. I couldn't have taught that lesson better if I had tried. I had been asking this particular employee to help us with her part of the work and flow. My mentoring efforts needed to catch up.

You could see that a light bulb went off in her head. She immediately saw what her work (or non-work) was doing to the organization. In the blink of an eye, she transformed from micromanaging her domain—a "this is my department, my work" perspective—to seeing her work as part of a more significant flow, process, system, and client-centered.

I don't blame her for not understanding her position in the total flow of this process.

Remember Maggie's "You have to give me an A" when she did everything but forgot to pay the employees in chapter 14? With a half dozen people at my door saying, "Jefe, no cheque," I could've flown off the handle about her not doing her job. The issue at that time was that her job description needed to be result-oriented. It was not any lack on the employee's part.

Whose failing grade was the payroll dilemma? Mine.

The sales administrator didn't need to be yelled at to get her job done, and she didn't need the foreman to fill in the gaps for her. She just needed to serve the teams around her like she would a client, which meant understanding their needs better.

This spontaneous interaction broke down departmental walls and fostered a sense of collective responsibility. The foreman's willingness to speak up created an opportunity for change, and the sales administrator's desire to learn and adapt resonated with others. The session itself demonstrated the power of shared knowledge and understanding.

Following this revelation, communication channels opened up organically. The sales department collaborated more freely with accounting and production. This communication is not just about fixing a specific issue but a broader mindset of mutual support and collaboration.

We also used that session as a template for future educational opportunities. It highlighted the importance of fostering an environment of open communication, shared knowledge, and mutual respect. Education didn't stop with knowledge transfer—it continued as a catalyst for positive organizational change.

Organizational Transformation

I knew what it was like to be on the other side of a transformation. Initially, I was on my own, trying to develop better systems and make them work. I needed help along the way, and my people did, too. They knew they could—and did—contribute to the company, and they needed to know that I also recognized and believed in their contributions.

When hierarchy is no longer a factor, owners are free to work for their layers of management rather than the other way around. A collaborative approach emerges, with guidance and systems training provided at every management level, where everyone is free to address issues and improve overall workflow.

In a client-centric working environment, where each department treats the other departments as clients, growth transcends the bottom line. This goes beyond the typical "cross-training" notion, which often turns into a "learn how to wear a lot of hats" expectation.

Systems knowledge and flows, the upside-down method, and the idea of a Circular Organizational Chart facilitate cross-departmental *education* centered on understanding how each department fits within a culture dedicated to serving the client.

Each department is vital at any given moment, and all of them work for the others in a symbiotic relationship, where each department views the others as clients. This approach ensures that everyone, from the owner to the employee, from sales to production to accounting, treats each other with the utmost time, effort, respect, and energy—just as one would a client.

Such a dynamic working environment catalyzes growth financially and for every individual within the organization. It creates a workplace where everyone is empowered to contribute to the organization's success.

An environment where everyone thrives.

To learn more with a Circular Organizational Chart template, click here or put the link in your browser for bonus material on my website: TomatoPasteLeadership.com/bonus.

CHAPTER 27:
Invest in Your People

"Don't wait. The time will never be just right."

—Napoleon Hill

In an environment of trust and safety, where systems work consistently, and everyone can show up fully and completely to run them—without fear of another person screwing them over—growth becomes an experiment that everyone can participate in.

In other words, career development is a signal of safety.

The Impact of Career Development

When you commit to developing careers, you show every employee that you value them and their future, whether or not they stay with your organization. Employees begin to think of themselves beyond their current roles. Often, they take ownership of their roles and their growth within them.

This is possible when you give systems control of the business. Your environment becomes safer and more reliable when you and your managers control your moods and stress.

Employees in that environment don't have to worry that you'll throw more work at them, jump on their case about unvoiced expectations, or spring some new, half-baked system on them out of nowhere.

Our school systems do not teach in a way that enables us to lead or become part of organizations like this. Sure, there are individual courses on leadership, accounting, economics, communication, and people development. I even see entrepreneurial programs in some schools now, but that's not the same as teaching business development, and it certainly isn't owner development.

Even though many companies in the US are small businesses, we need more foundational education to run and grow a business. Instead, we learn the best we can through years of experience and any help we can access.

For employees who were taught to find their place in an organization and do whatever needs to be done, it often means learning to emulate whatever the boss is doing.

This mutual unlearning and relearning led to highs and lows in my leadership journey and likely will for you as well. Some will fail even if you create an environment for employees to thrive. My advice? Keep investing in your people and this environment anyway.

Investing in the Right People

Once the values of family and education became ingrained in our business culture, employees would come to me and say things like, "Domenic, my boy is in a tournament this afternoon, and I would like to be there. I need some time off." They knew that they would have that time with their boy because, let me tell you, if my daughters had ballet practice and needed my help to drive or cheer from the balcony, I would move or get help with my non-critical work without skipping a beat. My employees knew that I wanted that for them as well.

This is why we are growing, and the value of family is beautiful.

Don't let me give you the impression that it was a free-for-all. These employees were dedicated to their positions. They knew

I would have a question: "Are there any critical parts of your position that must be done? If yes, how are you going to make that happen?"

They also learned that they could ask for help from their team, or if the tasks could wait without causing issues in the flow, they could come back later to finish the work.

Throughout this transformation, I worked to help our employees understand what we were doing, where we were going, and how we would get there.

The employees were hired for their values or wanted to transition with us. The ones who were part of the old guard thrived when they learned to hold clearly defined positions inside the organizational strategy of our growing company. They worked hard to become part of the strategy.

Our company's value of education helped all of us work out the systems, strategies, and values that made this kind of freedom and whole-life success possible.

Unfortunately, most people who worked for you before implementing your values and strategies will find it hard to make this transition and will likely not work for you afterward.

But the employees who get it will *get it*.

I did not want to micromanage my employees.

The employees did not want to be micromanaged.

We didn't just want to change.

We wanted to transform.

Managing Resistance to Change

While on my leadership journey, I tried everything within my limited knowledge to help my employees grow. I taught them, mentored them, and was empathetic to their fears. The hardest part was realizing that my job was to mentor the people who belonged and remove those who did not. The old guard who didn't want to change needed to be moved to other companies. Helping people move from one company to another can be one of the most challenging parts of being a leader.

Early on, an employee, I'll call her Carla, made it clear she was from the old guard. She had been with the company for over two years and was hired into a communications job. She was the hub of communication—emails, letters, mail, telephone calls—everything came through her.

This was a vital position; she was the first person a client would interact with within our company. I hired her before I used the hire-to-values process.

She worked hard and was very pleasant, but the value of learning and using systems was not in her makeup.

Carla wanted to avoid learning or growing in that position, especially using templates and systems. This led to others picking up her slack, an absolute no-no in our organization.

She despised coming into career development sessions. She couldn't see them as anything but reviews, which she expected to lead to more money every time. However, as soon as every position had a posted range of pay and associated results to achieve, we stopped giving raises based on tenure. You knew exactly what you could make within a role, and if you wanted more than that, you would need to change positions.

With no interest in taking on new responsibilities and growing frustrated with her position, Carla became one of the first I had to help another company.

Another from the old guard, I'll call her Pia, really tested my growing leadership skills.

When we ran orientation programs for old and new employees, we ran three sessions on positions. First, we taught them that a position had a result, strategic responsibilities, task responsibilities, and a pay range, whereas a job description only had tasks. Then, we taught them how to use the Organizational Chart and how employees could understand and see the many opportunities available through the positions on the charts. Finally, we taught them about the career development system that would get them where they needed to go via education and mentoring. I did my best to give everyone a fair shake.

So when Pia and I replaced her review with a career development session, she wasted no time when we got to the last section: what do you want to accomplish in the next few years? What projects do you want to achieve? Who do you want to be, position-wise?

She said, "Domenic, I have been here the longest. I was your second office hire. I believe I should be the office manager."

Immediately, I could sense there was a problem.

Still, I needed to make every effort to help her to a place that would work for her as well as the company, so when she told me which position she was interested in, we looked together at the results it required:

> Results Statement: To provide staff support for the acquisition and retention of clients for the company through the planning, evaluation, monitoring, and improvement of financial tracking, information technology, and administrative systems in a way that promotes an effective, smooth-running organization.

Then we looked at the Position's Strategy:

1. Evaluate the performance and results of the office's internal functions and procedures.

2. Recommend and develop improved systems, policies, and/or procedures for all internal systems.

3. Hire and train all internal staff.

4. Prepare and deliver performance review evaluations to all internal staff.

5. Provide input and assistance to the Management Team toward achieving the company's status objective.

6. Review and provide financial reports to the Management Team monthly.

7. Manage all internal processes to ensure a smooth-running operation.

8. Plan, implement, and regularly review the company's budget.

We could both see that the necessary skills were not in her toolbox, and I knew they never would be.

Instead of asking how to gain those skills, she repeated, "Domenic, I've been here the longest. I work the hardest. You are putting me in a corner."

No matter how much I tried to mentor her through this dilemma or how much I wanted to treat her like the client and serve her actual needs, she kept repeating the "hard work" and "longest employee" lines.

I finally explained that I needed to be responsible for the whole company, which meant hiring the best candidate. Each position worked within a department and for other departments, and we were all accountable for the entire company, not just ourselves.

It is vital to dedicate time and resources to mentoring the Carlas and Pias. Sometimes, both parties are happier when they move on to another company.

The Long-Term Benefits of Investing in People

Is investing in career development worth it, even if it doesn't guarantee buy-in or loyalty?

My partner didn't think so. His mantra was, "You will spend all that time and money, and they will just leave for better pastures. They will leave to start another business—maybe even compete with you!"

In most cases, after the old guard made their way out the door, my partner's thought process about employees leaving was wrong. Most chose to stay and grow with us because they preferred the benefits, wages, collaboration, and positions we offered compared to our competitors. The core values created a significant attraction for great employees.

Remember the PricewaterhouseCoopers survey, in which growth was the top value of employees? That was what we provided.

Still, a few left for competing companies—and they were great catches for the companies that hired them.

In those instances, I didn't think of them as competitors. I knew I could someday hire them as subcontractors and sell them used and new equipment from our sales/repair company. I knew they were technically sound, and we could rely on them as industry partners. They made our industry better. If you ask me, it was a great trade-off.

I remember when a worker, Gilberto, told me he was starting his own company. I was damn proud of him. He thanked me for giving him a job and a chance when he came to America.

I shook his hand, wished him good luck, and asked him if he wanted snow work.

With a big smile, he said, "Of course, Domenic."

He subcontracted with us successfully for two years and then eventually returned and asked me for his old job.

He said, "Before, I would just have to work and collect my paycheck. But with my company, I had to sell, do quotes, do the work, collect the money, pay vendors, pay workers, do everything."

He was squeamish about asking but relieved that I said yes, he could work in the organization again. He was professional while working for us and spoke to me face-to-face about leaving us. He was experienced as a subcontractor and is now asking for his job back.

I respect anyone who knows their limitations. Owning a business is only for some, and we were honored to have a great learner, a great worker, and a great man back on board.

I continued to invest in employees throughout my tenure with the organization. Later, I named the program Ultimate University and made it a core part of our environment.

Yes, I spent time and money to give my people adequate training. While they were working for me, I had better workers. When they left, I knew I had provided something for their future.

An owner who dares to teach and mentor is not worried about losing their investment in training and education when employees move on to other companies or start a business. They are also not concerned about controlling their employees during a transformation. The values, systems, and mentoring ensure everyone can take ownership of their roles.

Usually, our biggest fear is that we'll lose our identity if the company can succeed without us. Empowered owner-like employees become such a threat to this kind of owner that they trap themselves in a worker-owner mentality rather than facing their fears and learning to trust.

In that instance, values and purposes are our safety net. They give us something to anchor beyond the ego of being in charge. Otherwise, it can be almost impossible for a leader to release the reins.

The more you learn to trust the people you hire, the more confident you will be that your Purposes in Life will be met.

Investing in your people freely, generously, and intentionally can lead to the success you've always dreamed of. Trusting your team and fostering a culture of growth and development creates an environment where everyone can thrive.

Tomato Paste: The Final Product

"Day by day, what you choose, what you think, and what you do is who you become."

—Heraclitus

Imagine this journey toward leadership as though you're crafting the perfect recipe—a culmination of personal growth, interpersonal changes, and strategic business development.

The ingredient of Purpose in Life uncovered the anchor holding you to your life's path and ensuring you live the life you dream of. Now that you know your purpose and what you value in life, you can live with intention and create more success.

With the ingredients of your Strategic Objective and Company Values, you created a blueprint for your business, charting the course toward realizing your dreams. You know where you're going, how you will get there, and why your company exists.

You also built an Organizational Chart with positions within it so everyone could see where they fit in on that journey. This ingredient provides clarity to help you hire people on shared values journeys who are the best fit to propel your teams forward.

Next, you create opportunities for those employees to transform from workers collecting paychecks to genuine parts of your team, and you're happy to invest in them through orientation and career development.

These foundational concepts can be transformative all on their own, helping you live and breathe values and strategy after a career spent trying to command and control your way to success.

They also pave the way for system development to transform from a prescribed set of steps in your Playbook into a companywide Operation Manual filled with processes, templates, and company flows. These form the backbone of your delegation ingredient, which will free you and your team from the shackles of micromanagement.

Again, you could stop here and be assured of growth, enhanced systems, and increased profits. I don't know about you, but I felt like there was more.

Running a business needs to be a profitable venture. Running a successful business is also about creating an environment where everyone thrives—where their success extends beyond a paycheck.

The tools introduced to you in this book aren't just for personal prosperity. They're the building blocks of a collaborative organization of many, where everyone is part of the whole, instead of a company that requires you to run everything.

In these last chapters, we'll unravel the synergy between leader, employee, and system development and the ingredients we've named within each.

At this stage, owners always ask me the same questions: when will the employees make this change? When can I step back and let them run the systems? When will I see the company's transformation? There isn't an easy answer as to how your chicken-and-egg scenario will play out.

The truth, not the simplest but the only one that matters, lies within you.

When will you shift from a worker-owner to a mentor-leader?

You now have all the ingredients; let's explore how to combine them.

🍅 Key Concepts

- **Personal and Professional Alignment:** Aligning life and business brings life values together with business strategy. It is the cornerstone and crucial for a purposeful and successful life.

- **Organizational Structure:** Leadership structures—such as Purpose in Life, Strategic Objectives and Company Values, and Organizational Charts—provide a foundation for effective business management. They help a leader guide the business toward sustainable success.

- **Transformational Leadership:** The heart of transformation is the shift from a command-and-control mindset to a value-driven, collaborative leader with a visionary approach.

- **Continuous Growth:** Learning and striving for a mentor-leader role in the organization is a constant improvement process.

- **Finding Your Purpose:** What matters most is a future filled with abundance, prosperity, and unwavering presence.

CHAPTER 28:
Are You Open for Collaboration?

"Not everything that is faced can be changed, but nothing can be changed until it is faced."

—James Baldwin

Remember that epic snowstorm meeting at the beginning of the book?

Julio's grin at the forecast of up to four feet of snow was more than excitement about a winter wonderland. He was excited to show me their art. He knew that my presence used to be required during such weather events. He also knew that the systems were humming this time, and the team had it all under control.

Even before my coffee cooled, I vividly recall Mina asking, "Do you need to be here?"

She was right to ask. The collaboration couldn't have run any smoother and didn't require my meddling. But while I savored this moment of collaborative success, my partner clung to the facade of dominance.

He had sat at the table just as Mina told me, "WTF are you doing here? You shouldn't be here. Don't you have something else to do?"

Oh, boy. He was appalled and asked me to come to his office immediately. He had things to say.

"Domenic, you let her walk all over you. You should have asserted your authority as the man in charge. How dare she? You are the owner."

He thought that his pride should be the same pride and bosshood.

But you see, I wasn't hurt. I was prouder than ever.

While my partner wielded power through ownership, my strength came from the artistry of collaboration. The employees knew what they did in this organization mattered—for the client, the company, and themselves. They wanted me to see and feel that accomplishment, and I did.

The storm was a testament to our collaborative prowess, a feat that some of the consultants we employed at the time found mystifying and even my partner struggled to comprehend.

Was it magic, like the Nico-blue flower project or the pansies on Good Friday? No, it was something more.

Ironically, I felt more "in control" with a well-coordinated team than I ever did in a command-and-control mode. My partner, oblivious to the processes that provided this control, prioritized sales and contracts over collaboration. He didn't know anything about the company's flows and processes, but little did he know he was mentoring values to those who reported him.

Looking back to chapter 26 and the educational meeting that transformed our sales administrator's view of her role, my partner's management methods and commands introduced the problem. Our collaboration resolved it. She would send contracts as fast as she could—even if they weren't completed yet—because it made her look good in my partner's eyes. Everyone after her, like the foreman who'd had enough of the corners she cut, didn't see things the same way.

If you remember back to chapter 7, his chaos value also influenced my Liaison Manager, Mina, to stack her papers up and "look busy" whenever he was around. His assistant could barely sit through education sessions without being called to deal with something he needed her to manage.

Even this was better than the alternative—the one time he sat in on an education session with us, it was a disaster. While we were brainstorming, whenever I opened my mouth, I would get scolded. After an hour of lambasting us with, "Why don't all of you already know this stuff? You all should be doing this already," he stormed out as a proud owner.

While the rest of the team was busy treating everyone like a client, my partner and a few people under him missed the memo.

I closed the session with some humor: "Did everyone get that? I guess he told us how he feels!" We never invited him to a system meeting again.

I had known we were misaligned since that day when the conference speaker gave us the "shhhhhh" and said that the company was a facade of success. It was not okay, yet my partner was okay with that.

Like the rest of the team, I let that facade be how things ran over time.

Internally, I called this facade the "Pulling Back the Curtain" System.

We found that we could let my partner come in whenever he wanted, guns blazing, and hand whatever he needed to be done to anyone who walked by. If the cleaning lady were in front of him when he needed a proposal done, she would get the job.

Yet even the cleaning lady knew how the curtain worked. The curtain was pulled back, and our facade of "I am boss; hear me roar" work was given out. We would smile and nod. "Yes, sir, Mr. Owner. No, sir, Mr. Owner."

Let him bluster and billow and blow a gasket.

Then, when he left satisfied, the curtain would close as he returned to his king's tower, and we would return to our systems. The person he gave the task to would give it to whoever was responsible, and the system flow would be back on course.

"Shhhhhh," my favorite speaker from the conference once told me.

It was a different "shhhhhh," but an effective one.

I don't say any of this to disparage my partner. I needed to transform myself and the business and found the way to this transformation. He was my partner and an integral part of the company, but he was the old guard. You can't fire a partner as much as you might like to.

You must remember that you can command and control to a certain level. Our command-and-control level was $2 million in sales, but only collaboration would work at $15 million in sales.

Sustainable growth does not happen with partners who have different values. I see this play out in many other businesses. So many owners want to grow and make more profits, and they want the employees to do what they ask of them yet do not seek leader transformation. Some cling to authority, even when it hinders collaboration and stifles growth.

I coached one owner who included education and employees as the company's heart in his Company Values. However, just like Ben & Jerry's, it was nothing more than a beautiful wall decoration. In our infrequent education sessions, he would take my old partner's tactic and yell out empty "should," "why haven't you," "I am passionate because I care," and "just do better" statements.

Saying you believe in employee development but not giving them the time and space to develop hurts the employees first.

When the employees get fed up and leave, the business hurts, too.

The last organization that I built crumbled after my buyout and exit. It could not be managed as I built it when the owners returned to a command-and-control method. Positions were eliminated. Collaboration dissipated. Systems faltered. Benefits were removed, and leaders reverted to owners who were there for profits only. The once value-driven entity became a profit-driven venture, and a sharp decline in sales and profits followed.

I'm not saying collaboration is the sole path to success, though it is potent. You can increase profits while remaining in command and control, though this will be limiting.

I am saying that the tools we've discussed in this book are built to work within value-driven organizations.

You have to be open to collaborating with the value-oriented people you say you want to bring together, or you'll never transition to become the value-driven organization these tools are meant to create.

CHAPTER 29:
Are You Profit-Driven or Value-Driven?

"It is like being in a dark room. You cannot see anything. Then you find and turn on the light switch and see what is in the room. You can never forget what is in the room, no matter what you do afterward—switch the light on or off."

—John G. Chiarella Sr., my dad and greatest mentor

A constant guiding force in my life, influencing my business decisions and how I've fostered personal happiness, has been allocating resources to my purposes and values. This pursuit encompasses all the time invested in learning through experiences and my financial commitments to consultants, books, courses, and workshops.

However, my leadership transformation and stellar growth in my organization didn't result from finding a hidden secret. They occurred when my investments became consistent choices and intentions.

Many business owners fall into the trap of allocating time to whoever or whatever is the loudest or offers the fastest reward. I caution against the dangerous path of building a life solely on that "whatever is the loudest" strategy.

Our choices breathe life into our strategies and values.

There will be constant demands from your business and your life. The challenge lies in deciding which choices and demands will be allocated to your most limited resource: time.

A Crossroads Tale

I once coached a husband-and-wife team whose business had reached the $5 million sales level. As expected, the company was running their lives. They were at a crossroads: continue the grind, revert to a manageable level, or forge ahead to the new heights they envisioned.

This is where I came in.

You already know where I started.

We delved into their whys, unraveling their Purpose in Life through a diagnostic process. These crucial initial steps gauged our compatibility in a coaching partnership and helped shape a strategic roadmap spanning three to five years. At the same time, my thoughts extended beyond their immediate success, envisioning possibilities for their transformations into model leaders.

Their collective desire? More family time.

Tired of being tied to the business grind, they sought better control, improved systems, and a workforce more accountable for their roles. Ah, accountability—another term tossed around by consultants like a magical elixir. Its practical meaning? Anyone's guess.

The husband worked in production, sales, and field duties, while the wife handled payroll, vendor payments, and the office. I stepped in with what I do best as the systems and people development orchestrator.

During one of our brainstorming sessions—those exhilarating moments when the system's foundations were laid, and the teams brainstormed about departmental workings—the owners and sales, production, and accounting teams convened to craft a work order with an invoice system.

After the meeting, one owner pulled me aside and proposed an additional personal life strategy session with her and her husband.

A room adorned with the new system flow suddenly became the backdrop for a candid dialogue. The duo's wife fearlessly asked her husband a pivotal question.

How was his transformation progressing?

The room vibrated, and time seemed to stop with the impact of that explosive question. Uncertain I should partake in such an intimate discussion, I offered to leave. To my surprise, the wife insisted I stay, seeking my assistance.

From my vantage point, she was demonstrating remarkable leadership growth. We had been working through our leader development sessions, and she understood how creating systems, developing people to run those systems, and becoming a more effective mentor were all steps that were moving her toward her purpose.

Yet she sensed her husband's reluctance to relinquish command-and-control ownership. Despite professing family as his top priority, he struggled to balance business growth with family responsibilities.

We discussed four distinct levels of financial success in the life of a business, each with its nuances and challenges.

Level 1: Command-and-Control Success

- In this stage, you're the sole driver of your business. You handle every aspect except for possibly hiring production, service, or office support. The company and its profits are solely yours.

- Your time and resources are fully stretched, as are your profits. The gross sales in these businesses typically stay under $1 million.

- Eighty-seven percent of businesses operate at this level.

Level 2: Systems Upgrade Your Business

- This phase marks a shift toward organizational efficiency. Being more organized leads to increased profits, so your focus shifts to ensuring the consistent operation of systems.

- In my experience in landscaping and snow removal industries, companies break the $1 million sales barrier at this stage.

- Statistically, 7 to 8 percent of small businesses reach $2.5 million in sales. However, many face chaotic management challenges around this level.

- While reaching Level 2 is exhilarating, the previous command-and-control management style starts to break down. Time, profit, employee, and client management require a different approach. Changing your leadership style becomes essential for sustaining upward momentum. Alternatively, returning to a sales level aligning with your management style is an option.

Level 3: Value-Driven Growth

- This phase marks a fascinating turn in business dynamics. As systems efficiently operate the company, growth takes a significant leap when value-driven employees collaborate to run these systems.

- Statistically, 3 to 4 percent of businesses achieve $5 to $8 million in sales at this stage.

- The transformation into a leader is pivotal here as you hire and mentor based on shared values. Shifting from a command-and-control owner-worker to a collaborative manager becomes essential for sustained growth and success.

Level 4: Visionary Leadership

- This is a rare echelon in which systems autonomously drive the company, employees effectively manage these systems, and visionary leaders mentor their teams to success.

- Venturing into this level might be unnerving, especially when you notice few or no counterparts. It challenges you to question whether you're on the right track or if it's time to explore a less-traveled path. Forging ahead requires proactive commitment.

- Only 3 percent surpass $10 million in sales. Here, the leader transforms into a visionary. Mentoring values and imparting knowledge of systems and flows become central, carrying a vision that extends beyond the owner's profits to benefit everyone involved.

Without the influence of mentors and my wife's unwavering support, I might have retreated to the conventional path before reaching Level 4. The option to return to familiar, manageable territory exists at every stage, and it's usually a safe choice.

In the case of our crossroads couple, from the wife's perspective, her husband was clinging to the command-and-control level, and she was worried he was not letting go. In the ensuing dialogue, she laid bare her heart. She spilled out two decades of dedication—ten years building the business and the subsequent ten running it and raising a family. She craved more from life, the company, motherhood, and marriage. With mechanisms in place for change, the husband's continued inertia cast doubt on the likelihood of his transformation.

I knew what it felt like to be where both partners were. I used a lot of my energy, talent, and time to grow my business—and I took plenty of that time and energy from my family. Yet, as a coach and speaker, I've been asked for that elusive magic pill to propel owners into transformation. It is like leading a horse to water; despite serious attempts, you cannot force an owner into change.

As our emotional meeting ended, clarity emerged. Both owners knew they needed to distinguish between business and family, and the husband knew that his absence required deep reflection and change.

The crux of this transformation lies in his actions, not just his words.

Navigating Success: The Unsettling Truth

Sometimes, the challenge we have to navigate is presented by an owner's success—or just one indicator of success: financial.

With one such client, I was in the delicate position of telling him his success could have been optimized. There was more to it than money; he still needed to access it.

His response was a vehement defense of his achievements—a $3 million company, two homes, a beautiful wife, and two kids. According to him, he could buy and do anything he desired.

How dare I question his success?

He added, "If you think I'm unsuccessful, then F you, Domenic."

Okay, that went over well.

Yet, as a coach committed to creating change, I pushed forward.

He had documented his values and purposes with me, with his top Purpose seemingly being his beautiful family. However, the misalignment between his professed values and time allocation revealed a stark truth. When I asked him to rate his *fulfillment* of the family Purpose, he admitted he had reached a mere four out of ten.

Confronted with this misalignment, he finally acknowledged dissatisfaction with his current state.

Monetary success dominates most owners' aspirations (I, too, have been guilty of this). Success can and should transcend monetary gains.

Despite his family being a stated value, this client's energy overwhelmingly gravitated toward amassing wealth.

As a coach, I wonder whether someone's values and actions align. I wonder whether their true purposes were articulated or if "family first" is a script they think they should follow. Either way, when Purpose in Life is mere rhetoric without aligning choices and resources to realize it, the rest of the tools will also fall apart.

Navigating Challenges: Aligning Aspirations with Actions

My experiences with these business owners are not isolated; many business owners encounter comparable challenges in their journeys. Entrepreneurs and business owners often express their aspirations for growth, visualizing themselves at the pinnacle of great organizations. Their dialogue always involves a commitment to employees, the pursuit of excellence for themselves, and the grand announcement that their toil is all for their families.

The danger for these clients is that they unconsciously allocate their resources toward immediate accomplishments. Whatever is right in front of them usually lands in their business, even when they aren't in the office.

There is a personal toll exacted from such pursuits. Mine was marked by my daughter's innocent observation, "Daddy, you are on the phone all the time."

Sometimes, an external voice is needed to help us see the misalignment between our professed identity and the reality of our actions.

Balancing growth ambitions, employee welfare, and familial responsibilities is not easy. A central theme emerges: aligning your choices and the resource of time with your Purpose in Life is not just desirable; it's vital.

Sharing Values (and Profits) with Employees

My journey to write this book began during the hibernation months of the COVID-19 pandemic when I joined Seth Godin's Akimbo Writing Workshop. During this six-month program, Ted, a fellow creative, and I engaged in an insightful conversation about nurturing a company's greatness beyond mere financial gains.

He asked me, "Domenic, does this transformation you advocate for benefit the employees? I read your stories and can see where the owner benefits. Yet I can only imagine the questions that echo in the employees' minds during growth discussions."

This is an excellent question that I am often asked, and it resonates with me. I know all too well the familiar narrative of profit-driven companies thriving at the expense of their workforce.

I get it. We can all acknowledge that many companies retain profits for the exclusive benefit of owners and partners.

Growth paints a different picture for value-driven companies. These leaders don't have to be questioned by employees about whether they'll share in the company's success. Employees know their importance, trust the owners, and excel in a safe environment. I have witnessed this in my organizations and the ones I have coached through this transition.

However, employee skepticism often prevails—especially from the outside looking in and especially in the early stages of transformation. Employees, even those well-compensated, can find it hard to trust a shift in the owner's approach. The scars of past experiences of being "cogs in the wheel" linger. Talk is cheap, and so are most owners.

Let me summarize my response to Ted's inquiry and some relevant insights.

This leadership journey spans twenty-seven years of growth as a landscape/snow company owner. My value of hard work initially shaped it during high school and college. What I loved most then was that the job financed my college education.

In our growing years, my partnership allowed me to support a family. Of course, we were driven by profits. With sales of just under $1 million, we deemed it a successful business model.

Fast-forward a decade. We surpassed the $1 million mark, confronted challenges at $2.5 million, and then stagnated briefly at $5 million before propelling into the top 3 percent of the industry. Ultimately, we reached $15 million in my final seven years.

Looking back on the struggle to break the $1 million sales barrier, it was easier than it felt at the time. Add a few systems, and voila. We flew to the $2.5 million mark, where more clients, payroll, equipment, trucks, loans, office work, sales work, and headaches started to take a toll on us.

Why a toll? The systems, pivotal as they were, fell short. Employees needed training and value alignment, which we still needed to name. Fundamentally, our reluctance to relinquish control hindered our progress, and employees mirrored what we had molded them to be.

The shift from the $2.5 million to the $5 million level came as we hired based on values. Employees aspired to do something more significant. With trained individuals who embraced systems, we morphed into a cohesive, functioning team. The business transformed from a mere entity into a thriving organization.

This transformation wasn't just a shift in systems and employees but also a personal evolution from worker-owner to leader.

It took a while, but I embraced Zig's philosophy: "You can have everything in life you want, if you will just help other people get what they want."

Success comes when you aid others in achieving their aspirations.

This transformation happened in my company when my employees were comfortable and trusted me as a leader. At that point, they transitioned from job holders to career builders, and we prioritized their career development. The following years were marked by growth and an expansive sharing of that success with our employees.

We were a collaborative group bound by shared values, collectively serving our clients. Our employees knew their roles were intricately connected to precise results within a comprehensive five-year growth strategy. They had a clear path through the Organizational Chart, supplemented by benefits such as health insurance, 401(k), profit-sharing, educational programs, and upgraded equipment. While working 24/7 for less than $1 million in sales, I scaled down to less than twenty hours a week while scaling up to $15 million in sales. Our financial success became a testament to our shared success, and it aligned with my Purpose in Life.

Our collaboration thrived because employees recognized their organizational roles and were offered meaningful work and purpose. Their contributions were as integral to the company as the benefits and pay were to them. This was not just a workplace but a thriving environment marked by fairness and reciprocation. Growth wasn't merely about money; it encapsulated an employee's holistic experience within the company.

Generating profits is commendable, but my preference lies in amassing wealth collaboratively with good people who share in the prosperity of a company rooted in family and community values. By intertwining financial success with shared values, my organization transformed into more than a business—it became a family.

Everyone has an innate desire to be part of something more significant. What commenced as my venture evolved into a collective pursuit. I aspired to assist people in realizing their life purposes and passions. My employees' professional and financial success echoed in their return to their families, and they were proud of their achievements.

How about you? Are you aligning with your values in life and business?

CHAPTER 30:
Embrace the Process

"Most people rush after pleasure so fast that they rush right past it."

—Søren Kierkegaard

Ever heard someone say, "I'm lucky to do what I love"?

It's not about luck; it's a choice we all deserve to make.

Often, we dwell on the reasons things won't work, all of which seem entirely valid: We are too old to change, we have no time to build, we do the work, we have too much intense competition, there is too much government regulation and taxes, we do not have enough money, and many other genuine concerns.

These are all reasons not to do something; you can live in the truth of those limitations. Most will. But you will get nowhere by doing nothing.

I use this analogy with my clients, students, and family: When making any life or business choices, hold up the ten fingers of your two hands and give nine fingers to explain why something won't work. I know those nine fingers or reasons are factual statements, yet I choose to look at the one finger where it may work.

Looking at the one or two possibilities, not the eight or nine impossibilities, will set you apart. It will get you to your Purposes in Life.

The world is a vast canvas of possibilities open to us all.

Seeing the world as open, beautiful, and full of possibilities—and then stepping into one of those possibilities, no matter how difficult it might seem—may be the most challenging choice, but it is the most rewarding.

The Choice to Transform

My life journey, three businesses, and, later, my latest organization—coaching teams and business owners—helped me evolve into the leader I aspired to be. It began with my choice to be with the daughters I wanted to raise and my wife, who has inspired me. They are why I wanted to align with the natural laws of life, health, and abundance.

They prompted the choices that consistently led me to abundance, happiness, and success.

Our choices shape our paths.

If you're a high achiever or a driven individual, focusing on what you love has likely brought you to where you are today.

When I ask, "Why do you want to grow the company?" it often feels like a jolt to the system because it calls attention to the choices you've made so far and the choices you will have to make to move forward.

Balancing family and business is difficult, especially when both rank high in your priorities.

Is it easier to go to work? Of course, it is.

Is it rewarding to see your business grow and prosper no matter what? Of course, it is.

Most of us need to realize that we spend more time than required on the results, which is not what matters.

Short-term success tempts us daily. Just create systems. Just train your employees. Just buy this software. Try this program. Hire this person.

Without a vigilant eye on our Purposes in Life, seemingly effortless choices can lead us far off course. Decisions that seem suitable for work might conflict with long-term happiness at home. Striking a balance feels like a daily battle.

The bad news is there are still no magic bullets. Few of the "easy" answers will lead to lasting success, and every theory (including mine) will have its limits.

The good news is everything you need to know and do is right there at your fingertips.

Success is living out your dreams, whys, and life purposes. It involves making clear daily choices. It is being there for family, building a business, and finding success in personal and professional spheres. Amid family moments, business endeavors, and time with friends, the struggle lies in returning to what matters most.

Once I understood success from the foundation of my Purposes in Life, I could always return to it, no matter how hard it felt or how far off course.

Success is family. It is mentoring, helping, and providing for and with others. Whether I have an industry-leading business, a thriving coaching business, a great morning cappuccino, or a good conversation around the dinner table every night, I can find that success whenever I decide to look for it.

Every day of this transformation, I have had clear choices—to be there to see my daughters' bright eyes and smiles, to be with them into young adulthood, and to give them more than I can imagine in the long run. I want to be with both of my parents in their last years, to take care of my favorite mom-in-law, to travel with my wife, and to spend time with my close friends.

Those are the things that matter to me. No matter how much I enjoy helping others in my business, I only feel good about it briefly if it takes away from what matters.

Too many friends, family, and clients have realized too late that working only for money doesn't create long-term happiness. I can't help them regain their time, but I hope I can help you avoid losing more of yours.

Before you return to the world, armed with this understanding and its challenges, remember the elephant in the room: the fear accompanying transformation. Fear pushes us toward the easy answers and away from the love of what we do. Fear of change, losing control, and incompetence.

The problem is that when you want to appear to have all the answers—even if it's a facade (Shhhhhh!)—you limit your leadership growth, which will limit your business' growth.

It takes courage to get out of our own way and grow.

That's not a matter of luck. It's a choice.

The Evolution of a Leader

Utilizing any tools I've provided in the previous chapters will help you grow your business, giving you more free time and profits. And isn't that what it's all about? I say yes and no.

Yes, if money is the goal. No, if you want to create art.

While transforming my business, I envisioned a well-oiled machine powered by robust systems, aligned strategies, and a value-driven team not unlike the one I just described.

But here's the truth: it was about more than just getting the processes and structures right. Bringing that vision to life required a personal evolution. From the moment I defined my Purpose in Life, I repeatedly learned that stellar results demand growth on both personal and professional fronts.

After returning to the basics, I could only bring together the pieces of the business puzzle (the leader, employees, and system development).

I took the time to build my life with Purpose in Life.

I took the time to develop a Strategic Objective for my company, infuse it with Company Values, and hire and retain employees based on solid Organizational Charts and Positions.

I took the time to build a team that could run that company through clear systems and mentor and develop them to do so.

While piecing together the journey that shaped these chapters, I contemplated the phase of growth between my initial, unclear notion of delegation and the finely tuned machine we eventually evolved into. I took a retrospective look at the company's path, the development of my employees, the partnership dynamics I was navigating, and my development as a leader. My editor surfaced some questions:

- When did the pieces of the business puzzle come together?

- At what point did you all begin reaping the rewards of your efforts?

- How did you know you were on the right path?

The answers were complicated and brought up more questions:

- Was hiring value-driven employees or educating seasoned employees more impactful?

- Did a turning point occur when our systems finally worked smoothly?

- Did our gradual shift toward more leadership-centric roles most affect our growth? Or did it happen when our employees exhibited a sense of ownership?

I wanted to say yes to all of the above until I finally realized *why* I wanted to say yes: Growth *was* essential on many fronts before we could ascend to the next level. That's why the initial years of this journey were a tumultuous ride of growth, system implementation, and relentless effort.

We were all growing at different paces.

It wasn't just me and my employees who struggled with this transition. I remember hearing some backhanded suggestions at conferences, too. One speaker was a consultant who said we needed to "have more courage" at the delegation stage.

Let the people run the systems.

Have more patience.

Trust the process.

Just do it.

Do you "have more courage"? Let the people do the work. Let me know when we make more money; everything will be hunky-dory.

The truth was, I couldn't yet trust the systems to do the work.

I couldn't trust the people to run the systems or the company.

Not right there and then.

And they didn't trust me.

It was the chicken and egg again. I was a big chicken waiting for the egg to get moving.

If only I could go back to give myself my advice (and a bit of an actual backhand): "Hey, Domenic, are you taking stupid pills? You want to change the employees, but what about you and your crazy-ass partner?"

It's challenging to make the new way consistent throughout the company and to let go of the reins. The hardest part is teaching your employees an owner-like mindset when you're just learning to be a leader instead of an owner-manager. It's also difficult to earn their trust.

I needed more courage to take the first steps in this brave new world I wanted to create for and with my people, but I also needed to finish creating the environment in my world to do that.

Retaining a command-and-control method might have produced compliance, but true collaboration demands a different approach. To forge a collaborative company, the leader must give orders and inspire. Then, we can lead our people toward the promised land of collaboration, innovation, and shared success.

The chicken needed to cross the street.

I believe that success is not an individual endeavor. It is created by a team with a singular vision through the collaboration of everyone's genius.

Cultivating Excellence: A Legacy of Tomato Paste Leadership

We host directors of internships from the University of Connecticut and Naugatuck Valley Community College every spring and summer.

We benefited significantly from these young minds' invaluable untapped knowledge. I loved including them in meetings and involving them in our company's growth. We would put them in a mentoring position and create projects for each department. Their infectious, can-do attitudes and unbridled enthusiasm injected fresh energy into our workplace, offering candid collaboration that lifted the spirits of my seasoned team.

They were just young and unaware enough not to see the limitations that can often shackle experience. I loved this about them. They didn't know it was impossible.

When the program started, I would walk the directors and assistants through each department and introduce them to the staff and employees. Six people were in the office, five in the production room, three in the greenhouse, and five in parts/ repair. Managers and employees would tell the directors about their positions and how they worked, and the directors looked over the large scheduling boards that placed over thirty-eight crews in the field.

This annual ritual provided the directors with a firsthand look at the bustling activity within our facilities and usually left a lasting impression.

During one such tour, one of my favorite directors from UConn posed a question that resonated: "Domenic, how do you keep so calm while managing so many departments and people?"

I was happy to explain to her that it only looked like I was running everything. I let her in on my secret: my calm exterior was a product of relinquishing the ego of knowing everything. The real heroes were the dedicated employees steering each department.

It wasn't about relinquishing control but embracing collaboration—a true sense of calm was born from self-command, not command over others.

My weekly meetings with department managers were mentoring sessions, not micromanaging sessions. My teams knew they could come to me for the most challenging problems. Our collaborative sessions delved into problem-solving, mentoring, system improvements, and visions for the future.

For everything else? I wasn't needed. The employees loved their strength as much as I did.

Let's revisit the pre-snow meeting.

Julio, the production manager, loved doing what he was doing; you could see it. He was in charge of his production department and his position. He knew I would be there for him if he needed me, but I could see the "I got this, boss" mentality in his eyes.

In the sales/repair department, Mick kept up with the daily details of all the equipment and truck management. He trusted that I'd back him if something came up.

Mina could smirk at me, "Dom, what are you doing in this meeting?" whenever she wanted. Yet she controlled her position and department well—dare I say, better than I did in that position.

Errors marked my journey, but each one fueled my progress.

In the beginning, I had a massive fear of being wrong. Eventually, I realized that I could learn something from everyone I met. Encountering new information gives us a choice: We can keep our previous opinions and stubbornly stand our ground or commit to pursuing new ideas—even if they prove our views wrong.

Eventually, it didn't matter if I could prove anything to anyone anymore—I wanted to improve myself and see how good I could get.

I welcomed challenges, appreciating those who challenged my perspectives. Pursuing truth became my compass, even if it meant being proved wrong. My executive coach's wisdom (is calling me asshole wisdom? I think so) illuminated my path: being wrong isn't a setback but a stepping stone to the correct answer.

Knowing that being wrong was a pathway to being right, I could make better, more precise decisions.

That's how I knew when to correct my path and sell my partnership, even though I was at the top of the game.

My ideal exit included a few other potential paths. I could have the employees take over, create a legacy for my children and have them take over, or merge with a larger company.

Truthfully, I wanted my employees to buy me out instead of exiting early like I did. Whether I sold to the employees, created a legacy for my children to take over, or handed the business off to a larger company, I needed to develop a valid business that could run independently without me being there.

All along the way, I needed to have each department systemized, each position ready, and all our delegation materials and education organized. I had to be prepared to let go at a moment's notice.

That can be a goal for us all. No matter your power, you can't keep it forever.

I held an unwavering commitment to let go when the time was right—acknowledging that no one can hold onto power indefinitely.

When the business took a corporate shift without me, compromising the company's familial essence, it was time to move on.

Your values are not achievable; you can only pursue them. For a guy who likes control, that's a challenging concept to accept.

Purposes like "family" can only be part of my life when I intentionally and consistently incorporate them: helping my daughters move to another apartment, spending time with my mother-in-law, traveling with my family and friends, and guiding my daughters when they ask (and sometimes when they don't).

Purpose in Life is enduring. It can't be checked off a list, achieved, or won.

Short-term achievements can be deceiving in pursuit of enduring Purpose in Life.

My collaboration with my business partner was an example of deceiving ourselves. Our purposes, profits, and growth were an easy path to immediate financial success. Yet we had to navigate the complexities of our misaligned intentions and minefields daily without seeing the long-term results.

The long-term results gave employees mixed signals between command and control and collaborative management. Another long-term result was the breakup of our company.

Sooner or later, misaligned purposes became too great to overcome.

Tomato Paste Leadership isn't about the fastest, cheapest solution. It's about nourishing an organization with love, care, intention, and joy.

Imagine what a hundred-year-old family recipe passed down through generations tastes like—jarred with love, care, intention, and joy.

As the sauce of life simmers, envision your company's future similarly: thriving on the shared processes and values handed down by respected leaders.

Imagine what your company would be like if it were filled with the best people, all working together with love and care. They would be focused on the processes handed down by leaders they trust and admire, working toward the same goal.

Imagine what that kind of company can do.

That is what Tomato Paste Leadership is all about.

Sure, you can settle for store-bought, mass-produced canned tomatoes. They might offer nourishment, make an okay pasta, and save you a few bucks. Is that all you want?

Remember, there are no quick fixes—just better choices.

That's the only way to overnight success, like me and our organization, even if it takes twenty-seven years.

Conclusion: Finding My Purpose in Tomorrowland

"The one who plants trees, knowing that he will never sit in their shade, has at least started to understand the meaning of life."

—Rabindranath Tagore

In the introduction, I asked, "What does it take to be a leader and grow a great company?" One that is meaningful to the client, the employees, the community, your family, and you, the owner.

The answer was simple: I wanted to be with my family.

I also wanted:

- Freedom to live and work the way I want.

- To create a company that shares my values and culture.

- For my family and community to be proud of me.

- To make a difference for my family and employees.

- To create a business environment where everyone thrives.

I wanted to be successful in the truest sense of the word.

As I pen these closing words, I marvel at my journey.

From the start of college, where I thought I would be an engineer, to partnering with my dad in our electronics manufacturing company and learning how to run a business.

From the spirited partnership with a second partner to becoming a family with my beautiful wife and daughters.

From leading a top three percent organization to discovering the three keys of leadership, employees, and systems.

From sharing my experiences in a vibrant coaching organization to teaching the Pyramid of Success framework.

Every step has been transformative.

My time with my beautiful wife and daughters, cherished memories with my parents and closest friends, built a business where everyone thrived, and each exciting venture weaved together a well-lived life.

"Success is not measured solely by profits and business accolades but also by the moments we share with loved ones and the positive impact we create in the world."

—Domenic A Chiarella

I have been where you are now. I often think about those times, sitting with my daughters as they painted their faces with Mickey ice cream bars. I know you suspect, as I did, that there is a more effective, profitable, and purposeful way to live, grow, and do business. Take it from my experience.

Take it from my daughters. There is a way.

I had a choice. I could have ignored Toni Marie, Rachael, and Jessica. But you already know what I did. I listened to my daughters and the part of myself that knew they were right.

Hard work just wasn't enough anymore.

What are you going to choose? What will your legacy be?

Take pride in your work, but know it may not be everything you do. If work and profits are your number-one priority—your baby in life—you may one day find that your real baby has left you standing alone, and money is the only thing you have left.

I know what I have in life and am committed to fulfilling my purpose before leaving this world.

As you close this book, I sincerely thank you for your time here.

Thank you for allowing me to share the experiences, insights, and tools that have shaped my life and business.

Please find inspiration within these pages to craft your unique journey toward a thriving and fulfilling life.

Remember, the journey doesn't end here—it merely transforms into your next chapter of growth and discovery. Embrace it with an open heart and a dedicated commitment to creating a life and business that brings you joy, success, and profound fulfillment.

Wishing you a future filled with abundance, prosperity, and the unwavering presence of what matters most.